# CONSERVATION HANDBOOK

🔱 BOY SCOUTS OF AMERICA

Library of Congress Catalog Card Number: 91-58676

Copyright 1991
Boy Scouts of America
Irving, Texas
ISBN 0-8395-3570-8
No. 33570    Printed in the U.S.A.

# Conservation Handbook
## by Robert C. Birkby

### Acknowledgment

Robert Birkby is a former director of conservation at Philmont Scout Ranch and is currently a chief instructor of the Student Conservation Association's Wilderness Work Skills Program. An Eagle Scout, he is the author of the tenth edition of the *Boy Scout Handbook*.

# Table of Contents

# Introduction

Wise stewardship of natural resources is the responsibility of all of us. The *Conservation Handbook* is a valuable tool for Scout leaders, parents, agency personnel, and others who realize the tremendous excitement and importance of involving young people in the care of the world around them.

# CHAPTER 1

# Rolling Up Their Sleeves

Across America something wonderful is happening. Scouts of all ages are rolling up their sleeves and going to work for the good of the environment. In the homes and communities where they live and on the lands where they camp and hike, Scouts are doing their part for a healthier planet. With youthful energy, joy, and plain old-fashioned sweat, they are improving their world.

Their efforts are good for land, air, water, and wildlife, and for the rest of us, too. What Scouts are doing is also of tremendous value to them. From Tiger Cubs through Explorers, they are discovering that they play a vital part in the quality of the environment. Scouts are seeing that they can make a real difference.

*Listen:*

That crisp autumn afternoon was a good time for the Cub Scouts to be outdoors, especially to have so much fun. The digging wasn't easy, but they kept shoveling until all of the holes were the right size. Then they carried small trees from the back of a truck and eased one into each hole. Making sure every sapling stood straight, the Cub Scouts pushed dirt around the roots and watered the soil.

The Cub Scouts had learned about planting trees when rangers from a nearby public forest had visited a pack meeting. They had told the boys how trees purify the air, give shade, and provide shelter and food for small animals. They had also suggested where the Cub Scouts could get young trees and where and how they could be planted.

After the trees were in the ground, the Cub Scouts checked them every week. They watered them when the weather was dry. They trimmed dead branches. When one tree began to grow crooked, they used padded wire and wooden stakes to pull the trunk back in line.

Over the years, the saplings became tall and graceful, but they weren't all that was growing. The Cub Scouts who had done the planting became adults who smiled whenever they looked at their trees reaching into the sky. They knew the trees were there only because of their efforts. The trees were proof that the boys' contributions to the environment had begun when they were very young.

## Listen:

In return for the good times they had enjoyed, a Boy Scout troop wanted to contribute to the upkeep of a park where they had often camped. The senior patrol leader and Scoutmaster met with a park ranger who suggested several conservation projects. A hiking trail needed maintenance and some eroded stream banks required repair. The ranger said she also hoped to conduct a census of migrating birds, reseed meadows damaged by overuse, and collect information on numbers of weekend visitors using backcountry campsites.

The troop leaders were most interested in the ranger's suggestion that the Scouts build a footbridge across a stream several miles up a trail. It promised to be a challenging task appropriate for the troop's skill level and time commitment. If the Scouts were willing to do the work, the ranger assured them she would have the materials for the new bridge delivered to the site.

The Scouts were excited to hear about the footbridge project, and decided to plan a campout as part of the project. When the time came, they backpacked to the stream and pitched their tents. With the guidance of their Scoutmaster and senior patrol leader, they assembled the bridge footings and put the long stringers over the water. The rustic design allowed the Scouts to use their knowledge of knots, axes, crosscut saws, and other hand tools. They were also able to practice leadership skills and group cooperation, and to fulfill several requirements for merit badges and conservation awards.

That night around the campfire, the Scouts reflected on the work they were doing and its importance to the land. They liked the feel of the tools in their hands and the sense of accomplishment in building a bridge. Because hikers would now stay on the trail across the bridge rather than sliding down the stream banks and disrupting aquatic habitats, the Scouts knew their work was enhancing the environment.

The next morning after a breakfast of pancakes and eggs, the Scouts nailed down planks for the floor of the bridge and installed hand

**Completing conservation projects helps Scouts realize they can play a meaningful role in protecting the environment.**

rails. The construction finished, they packed the tools and broke camp. They talked eagerly about future conservation projects they could do in the park.

Trail users were delighted to discover the bridge and were impressed when they read the small sign explaining who had built it. The ranger was pleased that the Scouts were becoming partners in caring for the land, and she looked forward to inviting the troop to take part in other conservation efforts.

For the Scouts, the project had been a weekend full of adventure. They'd had the fun of hiking and camping. Best of all, they had built something of real value. For years to come, they would tell people about *their* bridge. They would take their friends and families to see it. That hands-on conservation project had increased the environmental awareness and sense of pride of every one of those Scouts.

*Listen:*

An Explorer post eager to investigate careers in conservation invited professional resource managers to come to post meetings and share information about their work. Some were federal agency personnel who managed vast forests and wilderness areas. Others represented city departments responsible for clean air and water, for sewage and trash disposal, and for care of urban parks.

The young men and women in the post were amazed by the wide variety of jobs that address environmental issues. The more they learned, the more they wanted to get involved. In cooperation with agency personnel, the Explorers started planning and carrying out their own conservation projects. They began by building waterfowl nesting boxes, then canoeing down a river and installing the boxes at remote sites pointed out by a wetlands specialist.

In the months that followed, they recorded data about the birds using the boxes and gave the information to agency biologists conducting a waterfowl study. They also helped organize a neighborhood recycling program, and as their concern about conservation issues grew, they developed an environmental education exhibit and presented it for elementary school classes and at career fairs.

Agency professionals came to regard post members as enthusiastic partners in planning and carrying out valuable conservation work. For the Explorers, the environmental focus of their Scouting program was the source of good fellowship and enjoyable adventures. It also taught them a great deal about how they could serve their community, and it gave them a strong sense of *stewardship*—a deep commitment to being responsible caretakers of the Earth.

*Listen:*

During the past fifty years, half a million Scouts have backpacked into the rugged mountains of Philmont Scout Ranch in northern New Mexico, the BSA's oldest national camp. The impact of so much hiking and camping might have endangered Philmont's fragile alpine ecosystems, but on the whole, that has not happened. Forests and streams teem with wildlife. The campsites and trails are well-maintained. The land is healthy.

The successful protection of Philmont's environment is the result of very hard work. Scouts trekking at Philmont volunteer part of their time to complete conservation projects. Beneath the bright New Mexico skies, they may install water bars to slow hillside erosion, build rock retaining walls, and reshape trail tread. Some close and revegetate trampled campsites to give overused areas time to recover. Staff conservationists skilled in environmental education help Scouts appreciate the significance of the work they are doing.

Philmont's conservation program is a superb example of how those who use the land can also contribute to its well-being. It is a model being adapted by Scout camps across America. It is proof that hands-on projects combined with environmental education can ignite in young people the fundamental understanding that they have a critical role to play in caring for the environment.

Young people everywhere are hungry for the chance to make a positive difference in the world around them. Through Scouting, they are

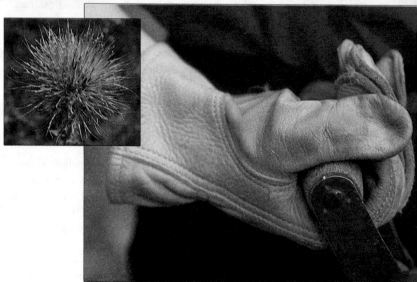

taking part in conservation projects that are exciting and satisfying to them, and very beneficial to the environment. They are planting trees, repairing meadows and campsites, building bridges, exploring environmental careers, and doing much, much more. As they wade in streams, haul rocks, recycle newspapers, and dig their hands deep into the soil, they are nurturing a personal concern for their own small corners of the environment that can flourish into a reverence for the Earth.

Many young people are already involved in conservation efforts. Many more want to do their share. Ready to take on all kinds of environmental challenges, they only need to know where to start.

This *Conservation Handbook* is a book about getting started. It is for everyone in Scouting, for parents, park and forest rangers, and other resource managers who want to involve volunteers in projects that are good for the Earth. While the manual bears the emblem of the Boy Scouts of America, its message is of value to leaders of many organizations. It is a book for anyone eager to explore environmental opportunities that will help young people grow and become wise.

# CHAPTER 2

# Conservation and the Scouting Program

Conservation and environmental education have always been deeply woven into the philosophy and program of the Boy Scouts of America. The ninth point of the Scout Law, *A Scout is thrifty*, offers a clear statement of Scouting's belief in responsible conservation practices. Here is how the *Boy Scout Handbook* explains the idea of thrift:

> *A Scout works to pay his way and to help others. He saves for the future. He protects and conserves natural resources. He carefully uses time and property.*

As a camper and backpacker, you will learn that you can live very well with no more possessions than the clothes you are wearing and the gear in your pack. As a Scout, you will also see that practicing conservation is a sign of thrift. Protect and conserve the Earth's natural resources—its soil, water, forests, wilderness areas, and wildlife. Recycle papers, glass, and metal used in your home and community. Waste is an enemy of thrift. When you act to stop it, you are doing your part to keep the Earth beautiful.

The Scout slogan, *Do a Good Turn Daily*, can apply to deeds done for the sake of the environment. Scouting's commitment to wise conservation practices is also expressed in the Outdoor Code:

---

*As a citizen of the world, I will do my best to—*
*Be clean in my outdoor manners*
*Be careful with fire*
*Be considerate in the outdoors*
*Be conservation-minded*

---

Scouting actively promotes environmental stewardship by teaching *low-impact* and *no-trace* methods of camping and hiking. Scout leaders also encourage young people to be conservation-minded at home, in their neighborhoods, and in all other aspects of their lives. Through its literature and program, the BSA fosters the idea of living in harmony with the environment rather than abusing it or trying to conquer it.

(See appendix 1 on page 110 for information about the conservation-related requirements for Cub Scout rank advancement, Arrow Points, and activities badges, and for Boy Scout and Explorer rank advancement and merit badges.)

## CONSERVATION AND THE *Boy Scout Handbook*

The tenth edition of the *Boy Scout Handbook* is a powerful tool for Scouting leaders interested in promoting environmental education and hands-on conservation projects in their unit programs. Here's how.

☆ Chapters on camping, hiking, bicycling, and other outdoor activities stress the use of no-trace and low-impact methods that are kind to the environment. They give Scouts and their leaders everything they need to know to enjoy the outdoors in ways that are responsible and wise.

☆ The chapter entitled "Using Woods Tools" (knives, saws, and axes) encourages Scouts to use these tools in ways that enhance rather than damage the environment. Mastering the use of woods tools can be an exciting part of the Scouting experience, especially when it is coupled with projects that allow Scouts to use axes and saws to complete conservation projects that are good for the land.

☆ The "Understanding Nature" and "Observing Nature" chapters invite Scouts to explore the wonders and complexity of the natural world. They remind readers that the environment includes every part of our world, from deep wilderness preserves to the urban rush of the inner city. The writing addresses natural systems and individual animals and plants in ways that help Scouts see the wonders and intricacies of the world around them.

☆ The section "Caring for the Earth" underscores all Scouts' responsibilities to care for the world in which they live, and emphasizes their opportunities to tackle environmental problems. Whenever young people help improve and protect a small corner of the environment, their sense of stewardship increases.

☆ At first it may not seem as though the "Democracy," "Community," "Family," and "Personal Development" chapters have much to do with conservation. However, each of these chapters can help Scouts better understand their role in decision-making, increase their willingness to accept meaningful responsibilities, and expand their realization that they have a real part to play in their homes, communities, and nation.

Young people who have little self-esteem may find it especially difficult to understand why they should work for the good of the environment. The handbook's "Personal Development" chapter encourages readers to recognize the talents they do possess and to take full advantage of opportunities to learn, to achieve, and to grow. Many Scouts will discover that becoming involved in environmental projects is a natural outgrowth of their efforts to make the most of their own lives.

# Scouting's Conservation Awards

BSA conservation awards honor the accomplishments of those who make significant contributions to protecting and enhancing the environment, and who are sharing their knowledge with others.

## HORNADAY AWARD

The Hornaday Awards program recognizes outstanding efforts involving environmental enhancement, natural resource conservation, ecological protection, and pollution prevention undertaken by Scouts and Explorers, leaders, Scout units, and others associated with the Scouting program. Originally known as the Wildlife Protection Medal, the Hornaday Award was established in 1914 by Dr. William Temple Hornaday, then director of the New York Zoological Park and founder of the National Zoological Park in Washington, D.C.

Hornaday Award recipients exhibit a deep commitment to conserving resources and improving the environment, and strong leadership skills in organizing and carrying out beneficial work. Projects worthy of consideration for the Hornaday Award must also increase public awareness of the need for adequate protection and management of natural resources. They usually take eighteen months or more to complete.

## TAKE PRIDE IN AMERICA AWARD

Begun in 1987, the Take Pride in America campaign is designed to instill in all Americans a strong awareness that public lands are their lands and that each person shares responsibility for what happens on those lands. The Take Pride in America Award is presented by government agencies to Scouts who have completed significant conservation work on public lands. Those who wear the Take Pride in America patch have shown by their actions their belief that every American has a duty to be a good steward of public lands.

## WORLD CONSERVATION AWARD

Boy Scouting and Exploring recognize the importance of environmental understanding by giving the World Conservation Award to those who earn merit badges for Environmental Science, Citizenship in the World, and either Soil and Water Conservation or Fish and Wildlife Management. The Cub Scout World Conservation Award goes to Cub Scouts who complete a selection of achievements, arrow points, or activity badges that lead to greater awareness of the world's environment.

## HISTORIC TRAILS AWARD

America's trails and archeological sites form a rich part of our national heritage. Scouts who wish to earn the Historic Trails Award must research the significance of a historic trail or site. To become familiar with it, they may hike and camp for several days and nights on the historic trail or in the area of the site. They may also work with adult leaders to protect the trail or site, make beneficial repairs, and further enhance the condition of the location.

## TRAIL BOSS

"*Teaching Resources And Individual Leadership*"—that's what TRAIL Boss is all about. It's purpose is to teach volunteer leaders of any organization the specialized skills they need for training and leading volunteer crews involved in conservation projects.

Instructed by conservation work experts from land management agencies, the BSA, and other conservation groups, TRAIL Bosses learn how to encourage and direct volunteers in completing demanding conservation projects on public lands. As these leaders gain knowledge and experience, the TRAIL Boss program may offer them opportunities to help train other leaders interested in directing environmental work.

BSA training, recognition, and leadership encourage
young people to care for the world around them.

# CHAPTER 3

# Environmental Explorations

All of us have difficulty caring for what we do not understand. If we don't know where our drinking water comes from, conserving water by shutting off faucets may not make much sense to us. If we've never thought about where our trash goes, the importance of recycling may be a difficult idea to grasp.

Environmental explorations offer Cub Scouts, Webelos Scouts, Boy Scouts, and Explorers simple, exciting ways to discover the richness and complexity of the world in which they live. As they learn about natural cycles all around them, they may also realize that they can choose to live in ways that are beneficial to the environment.

## A Backyard Environmental Exploration

A back yard, meadow, or other neighborhood outdoor area is a good location for Scouts of any age to enjoy a first environmental exploration. Let Scouts take part in choosing the place they want to explore and invite them to think about what they hope to find. You might encourage them to think of themselves as detectives solving the mystery, "What's going on here?" Or they could imagine that they are explorers wandering into new territory for the first time.

Given the chance, Scouts will make many discoveries on their own. A leader can help by suggesting questions for them to answer and promoting fresh ways of observing. For instance, in a backyard environmental exploration, you might ask Scouts to consider the following:

☆ What kinds of animals live in the back yard? Look closely in the grass, under bushes, on the bark of trees, and in the soil. Look down, up, and all around. Listen for the sounds of animals and look for tracks, nests, and other signs. If you have them, use a magnifying glass for a closeup view of insects and other small creatures and binoculars for birds and other animals further away.

☆ Write a list of all the animals you find. If you don't know an animal's name, make up a name that seems to fit. Try drawing pictures of some of them. Sketch a rough map of where different animals live. Look them up in a nature guide and find out more about them.

☆ What do animals found in a back yard eat? Where do they sleep? How does their size affect the way they live? Of what importance is the color of their bodies and the markings on them?

☆ Follow an insect, bird, or small mammal as it moves. What is it doing? Get down close to the earth for an insect's view of the world. Climb a tree and look at the yard the way birds view it. Imitate the ways that other animals move about, and imagine how they see, hear, smell, and taste their surroundings. What do humans have in common with these animals?

☆ Take a close look at the plants in the back yard. Try drawing the shapes of some trees and their leaves. Are the trees thin and tall? Pointed? Round? Crush a leaf between your fingers and smell it. What is the aroma like? Try to identify the plant in a nature guidebook and read more about it.

☆ Can you figure out where trees and other plants get their food and water? Do plants living in shaded areas appear different from those in bright sunlight? Are any parts of the plants eaten by animals? Are there ways that animals provide nutrition for plants?

☆ Make a print of a leaf by placing it on a hard surface such as the back of a clipboard. Lay a sheet of paper over the leaf and lightly rub the top of the paper with a pencil or crayon. The image of the leaf should appear on the paper.

☆ Feel the soil. Is it dry or moist? What color is it? How does it smell? With a spoon or trowel, dig a few inches into the soil. Is the deeper dirt different from that on the surface? What animals live in the soil? Can you find the roots of any plants? There is often as much living matter below the ground as there is on the surface.

☆ Sit quietly for a few minutes and listen. What sounds can you hear that are made by humans? What natural sounds can you hear? What does the wind sound like? If you can hear birds, mimic their songs. Make a map of the sources of the noises in the yard.

As you can see, an exploration is a chance for young people to involve all of their senses in the act of discovery. There is no need for rigid rules or goals, though having fun is a valuable incentive for any educational activity.

Before the end of each environmental exploration, remind Scouts to return the area to the condition in which they found it. Replace over-turned stones and logs. Restore sod that may have been lifted out for examination, and fill in any small holes that have been dug. Take nothing unless there is a planned use for it. Encourage Scouts to treat all environments with the same care they give campsites and trails by leaving no trace.

(Cub Scouts will find that environmental explorations are reinforced by the project and support pages in the Cub Scout and Webelos Scout books. Boy Scouts and Explorers will discover much related material in the environmental chapters of the *Boy Scout Handbook*.)

## Other Environmental Explorations

Environmental explorations that reach beyond back yards can effectively help Scouts learn about the ecology of their neighborhoods and communities and how it is affected by human activity. Explorations can show Scouts how natural systems are related to one another and how caring for one part of the environment can improve it all.

Most resource management agencies and many private businesses welcome groups of Cub Scouts, Boy Scouts, and Explorers. Call at least several weeks ahead of time to set up a visit. Special arrangements must sometimes be made so that Scouts do not interfere with normal operations and so that their safety can be assured.

Scouts may wish to set out on a series of related environmental explorations taking place over a period of weeks. For example, they could follow the path food takes to reach their tables, beginning with a visit to a farm, orchard, or dairy. On future trips, they might visit a food packaging plant, then a truck terminal, and the back rooms of a grocery store. With visits to a sewage treatment plant, a landfill, and a garden that uses composting, they can learn about various end results of the food production path.

Consider the following public utilities and private companies as destinations for environmental explorations:

☆ Water departments

☆ Dams and reservoirs

☆ Public works administration, environmental services department, or others in charge of parks and streetside trees

☆ City planning departments

☆ Sanitation departments

☆ Sewage disposal plants

☆ Landfills

☆ Recycling companies

☆ Power authorities

☆ Arboretums

☆ Community vegetable gardens

☆ Greenhouses

☆ Bakeries

☆ Soft drink bottling plants that use recycled cans and bottles

☆ Paper mills

☆ Auto wrecking yards

**Senior citizens can be important partners in neighborhood conservation work.**

Anticipation is an important part of any adventure. Heighten the enthusiasm of an environmental exploration by including Scouts in its planning stages. Boy Scouts and Explorers can work out the details of an upcoming environmental exploration and perhaps invite someone to come to a unit meeting to provide background information before the event. Cub Scouts can decide which of several places to visit first and what to take with them on each exploration. Everyone can discuss what they want to get out of a project. What will they see, smell, and hear? What will they learn?

Senior citizens can also be valuable sources of information about how the environment of a neighborhood has been altered over the years. They may have photographs of an area as it used to be. What has changed? What has not? Have the changes all been for the better?

Many senior citizens also have time to share with Scouts involved in conservation projects. Do not be shy about inviting older members of your community to share their experience, enthusiasm, and information with Scouts.

# CHAPTER 4

# Projects and Partnerships

Environmental explorations enable young people to see the importance of natural systems. Conservation projects give them opportunities to take part in the protection and enhancement of those systems. The hands-on nature of projects helps Cub Scouts, Boy Scouts, and Explorers realize that everyone can play a positive role in caring for the environment.

During their involvement with conservation work, Scouts who want to know about careers in conservation can learn from agency professionals. Scouts interested in advancement will also find many opportunities to pass requirements for Scout ranks and badges.

For Scout leaders, conservation projects can provide a meaningful focus for unit activities. For park and forest rangers and other resource managers, Scouts involved in conservation projects can serve as deeply appreciated volunteers eager to complete vital conservation work on America's public lands.

## Public Lands

Almost a third of the United States is in the public domain. Parks, forests, wetlands, prairies, recreation and wilderness areas, reservoirs, seashores—these are national treasures in which every American shares equal ownership. Each of us also shares in the responsibility of caring for these resources.

We all benefit from public lands. Most of the water we use comes from our public watersheds, reservoirs, rivers, and lakes. The air we breathe is cleaner because of vegetation in our parks. Lumber used to build our homes and schools may have been harvested in our national forests.

We can visit most public lands whenever we wish. Many Scouts have enjoyed family picnics in neighborhood parks, fishing in state lakes and reservoirs, hikes in federal forests, and campouts in wilderness areas.

While all of us share ownership in public lands, various agencies oversee the daily and long-range uses of those areas. The agencies may be branches of a city administration or of county, state, regional, or national government. Local agencies such as community parks departments may care for only a few acres. The largest, including the U.S. Forest Service, National Park Service, Bureau of Land Management, and U.S. Fish and Wildlife Service, administer tens of thousands of square miles of the American landscape.

Each agency was established with particular goals in mind. Some focus on enhancing the habitats of wild animals. Several agencies

**Cub Scouts, Boy Scouts, and Explorers enjoy all sorts of outdoor adventures. In return, they are volunteering to help protect and improve public lands.**

manage their areas so that the pristine beauty of wild country can be enjoyed by present and future generations, and the natural ecological forces can function without human interference. Other agencies seek a balance of protecting natural areas and permitting the prudent harvest of resources.

Most agencies provide access to public lands by building and maintaining trails for hikers, backpackers, horseback riders, and bicyclists. They may establish campsites, picnic grounds, and swimming areas. Many parks and forests have information centers introducing visitors to the ecology and history of a region. Special facilities and travelways encourage people with physical limitations to enjoy the outdoors.

Regardless of the scope of duties, every agency is also obligated to protect the quality of the environment of the areas under its jurisdiction. That's where young people can become partners in taking care of the lands in which they share ownership.

(For descriptions of the major resource management agencies, see Appendix 2 on page 117.)

## The Idea of Partnership

Boy Scouts, Cub Scouts, and Explorers are eager to help resource management agencies care for the environment. They want to become involved in projects that are good for the land, air, and water. They are enthused about doing their part in caring for natural resources.

Likewise, agencies throughout the nation are encouraging Scouts to take active roles in caring for forests, parks, waterways, and other public areas. Involving Scouts in conservation work can help agencies address many immediate environmental concerns. Even more important is the fact that hands-on projects can inspire young people to become lifelong stewards of the land.

A partnership between a Scout unit and an agency is very much like a friendship. It is based on mutual interests, needs, and shared trust. Like any good friendship, such a partnership may take time to develop. It will require energy to get it started and keep it rolling, and sometimes it may demand a large measure of patience.

But the rewards of a Scout unit/agency partnership can be remarkable. Rather than just being hikers and campers who use public lands, Scouts can become active caretakers of natural resources. A partnership allows agency personnel to share their knowledge and skills with young

# NATIONAL PARKS—BLUE  NATIONAL FORESTS—GREEN

BUREAU OF LAND MANAGEMENT—BROWN    NATIONAL WILDLIFE REFUGES—BIRDS

people. Over time, an agency may come to rely on Scouting as an essential part of its volunteer conservation program. Likewise, Scouts can look to an agency as a source of opportunities for conservation adventures, education, and service to the environment.

## WHAT SCOUTING CAN OFFER AGENCIES

Projects that involve young people in the protection, maintenance, and improvement of public resources allow agencies to complete conservation work that would otherwise be impossible due to budget and staffing restraints. Scouts can be especially helpful with efforts that are too labor-intensive for field management personnel to undertake.

A Scout unit can be a very mobile, dependable work force. Boy Scouts and Explorers are able to reach remote projects by foot, canoe, or bicycle. During multi-day efforts, they can camp near work sites. They can carry their own tents and cooking gear, and can prepare their meals.

Because Scout units also have their own leaders, conservation efforts involving Cub Scouts, Boy Scouts, and Explorers require a minimum of agency staff time. Of course agency personnel should meet with Scout leaders to plan projects and provide guidelines and standards for completing the work. Furnishing tools and materials may also be the responsibility of the agency, as well as evaluation to guide Scout leaders in future projects. Even so, a benefit of Scout/agency partnerships is that the time required of agency personnel need not become a burden to them.

## WHAT AGENCIES CAN OFFER SCOUTING

Conservation efforts made possible by agency partnerships can give Scouts an effective way to put into practice the environmental messages of the *Boy Scout Handbook*. Scouts proud of completing agency-related service projects will be increasingly interested in natural resources and in the agencies that manage them.

One of the premises of Scouting is to provide its members with appropriate role models. Most young people enjoy being around adults who can teach them skills, entrust them with responsibilities, and help them become better people. By working alongside Scouts, agency personnel can find deep satisfaction in sharing their knowledge, attitudes, and enthusiasm.

Unit leaders meet in advance with an agency representative
to plan their conservation project.

A hearty handshake at the end of a project seals the growing partnership
between a Scout troop and a ranger.

## FINDING AN AGENCY

Locating an agency interested in exploring a conservation partnership may be as easy as looking out a tent door. The trails that Scouts hike and the campgrounds where they stay are probably cared for by agencies or conservation organizations. When you go to a park or forest or other public area, ask officials there for the name of the person who can talk with you about doing conservation work. Many agencies have a coordinator of volunteer affairs experienced in working with youth groups.

Stores that sell camping gear or equipment for hunting and fishing frequently have information about local recreation areas and the agencies that administer them. Scout council and district offices may be able to suggest the names of agency professionals you can contact. Councils and districts can also put you in touch with other Scout leaders who have made conservation projects an exciting part of their unit programs.

For more agency information, look in the phone book under U.S. Government listings for the Department of Agriculture to find local phone numbers of the U.S. Forest Service. Check under Department of the Interior to contact the National Park Service, U.S. Fish and Wildlife Service, and Bureau of Land Management. The Army Corps of Engineers is a department of the United States Army. Other land management agencies may be located in state, county, and city government listings.

## HOW TO APPROACH AN AGENCY

Contact the agency that seems most appropriate for a partnership with your unit and find the people who can work with you on a local level. They may be volunteer coordinators, rangers, or maintenance workers, or hold other positions. Explain that your Scout unit would like to explore possibilities for doing conservation projects on lands managed by the agency.

Working with Scouts may be a new experience for agency people. They may be unsure what to expect of Scouts and uncertain as to what the Scouts will expect of them. That's all right. It is part of the process of getting acquainted.

If possible, provide agency people with a copy of this manual and a copy of the *Boy Scout Handbook* so that they can take their time reading about the Scouting program and the value of conservation partnerships.

Invite agency representatives to attend a Cub Scout, Boy Scout, or Explorer meeting or to come on a hike or other outing. That will give

An agency representative attends a troop meeting to meet the Scouts and learn about their backgrounds and interests.

them a chance to meet the Scouts and learn about their backgrounds, interests, and enthusiasm.

Scouts might also plan an environmental exploration to visit the agency's offices and allow people there to share information about their areas of responsibility and the pleasures and challenges of their jobs.

As a Scout unit and an agency become acquainted with one another, Scouts can volunteer to complete a simple conservation project that will take just a few hours of a weekend. That will let Scouts sample hands-on conservation work, while giving the agency an example of the

Scouts' ability to enhance the environment. The Scouts will also be learning valuable conservation skills and work methods that will make them even more effective with future endeavors. An agency that discovers it can depend on Scouts will be very happy to involve them in larger and more challenging projects.

As with any friendship, a partnership between Scouts and an agency is built on a foundation of trust. If you agree to tackle a project, then go through with it. Be on time. Keep your promises. Even if the work isn't quite what you had hoped it would be, encourage Scouts to do their best every time they go into the field. They will be proving to the agencies that they are capable and determined to complete what they begin.

# PLANNING A CONSERVATION PROJECT

No resource manager will be pleased to have a dozen Scouts or Explorers show up unannounced on a Saturday morning eager to "do some conservation." Clear communication between Scout leaders and agency personnel in advance of a project will minimize rude surprises to agency personnel and a disappointment for the Scouts.

Careful planning also allows Scout leaders and resource managers to shape projects that will be satisfying to Scouts, of value to the environment, and matched to the skills of everyone involved. Someone from the agency may come to a Scout meeting to help the Scouts select the work they want to do, or a Cub Scout leader, a Scoutmaster and senior patrol leader, or several Explorers and their post Advisor may go to the agency office to talk over conservation plans.

Leaders unfamiliar with a project location should visit the work area before the day the Scouts arrive. When Scout leaders and agency personnel look over a project site together, they can head off many problems ahead of time. The extent of the effort will become clear, as will needs for tools, materials, safety considerations, transportation, and special clothing or footwear.

It's also a good idea to select a backup project near the location of the primary work. Should Scouts finish the initial work more quickly than expected, they can move on to the second project. When weather, unforeseen lack of tools or materials, or other factors make the initial project inappropriate, the backup work may give leaders an alternative plan.

## WHAT MAKES A GOOD CONSERVATION PROJECT?

Cub Scouts, Boy Scouts, and Explorers undertaking conservation work are volunteering their time and energy for the good of the environment. A worthwhile project allows them to feel pride in what they are doing. It gives them a chance to learn or experience something new. Though the work may be hard, it should also be satisfying.

The following guidelines will help Scout leaders and agency personnel plan conservation work that serves the needs of Scouts, of agencies, and of the environment.

**Involve Scouts in All Aspects.** Feeling a sense of project ownership is very important to young people. Increase their commitment to conservation by involving them in planning a project, as well as in carrying out the work. After completing a job, Scouts should also take part in restoring the area to its natural appearance, cleaning and storing tools, and doing whatever else is required to tie up all the loose ends.

**Make Projects More Than Work.** Whenever possible, combine conservation efforts with other Scout activities such as a hike, a campout, a swim, or a nature walk with someone who can discuss the area's ecology. This will enrich the experience for everyone and also reinforce the idea that caring for the environment is a fundamental part of the entire Scouting program.

**Choose Reasonable First Projects.** First projects should be limited in scope and last no more than few hours or an afternoon. As Scouts gain experience and prove their worth in the field, projects can become more lengthy and complex.

**Consider Skill Levels.** A good project is within the skill levels of the Scouts carrying it out. Work that is too demanding sets up young people to fail and to lose interest in conservation projects. On the other hand, the best opportunities challenge Scouts to push a little beyond their current abilities and master new skills. Determining the difficulty of a project is an art that will develop as a Scout unit and an agency learn from their cooperation on each conservation effort.

**Safety.** An acceptable project can be done without endangering participants.

**Set Reasonable Goals.** Everyone likes a sense of completion to their work. Some conservation efforts can be finished in a few hours, an afternoon, or a day. Longer-term projects may be broken into intermediate goals achievable in shorter amounts of time—planting a certain number of trees, for example, or repairing the sites in just one area of a campground.

**Make a Difference.** Appropriate projects allow Scouts to see that their efforts have a positive effect on the quality of their environment. Leaders and agency personnel can enhance Scouts' satisfaction by explaining how the environment will benefit from the work. If they understand why their involvement is important, Scouts will usually be quite willing to put their energy into a project.

Agencies also have an interest in developing projects that are meaningful for volunteers. Scouts who believe they've played a genuine role in helping the Earth will be eager to come back for more. However, sticking young people with distasteful chores nobody else wants to do can kill that enthusiasm.

**Provide Variety.** A good project has variety. Doing different tasks during the day keeps the work fresh. Even repetitious projects can be broken down into an interesting series of steps—for example, digging plants to be moved for revegetation, carrying them to a new site, preparing the soil areas, planting, and hauling water. Scouts who spend time performing each of these steps will get a taste of the full project, learn about the effectiveness of the entire effort, and come away satisfied in having been involved in all phases of the work.

## Adopt a Site

Scout leaders can help members of packs, troops, and posts develop a strong sense of pride and ownership in their work through "adopt-a-site" partnerships with land management agencies. With agency support and guidance, a Scout unit can pledge itself to provide long-term care for a damaged campsite or meadow, or a section of a stream, lakeshore, or hiking trail. Over the years, Scouts investing their energy in their adopted project will be able to see how their efforts are improving the condition of an environmental area and protecting it from further abuse.

## Project Planning Checklist

Scout leaders and agency personnel can use the following checklist in their planning of conservation projects.

☆ What is the task to be done?

☆ Why is it important?

☆ How many Cub Scouts, Boy Scouts, or Explorers can take part in the work?

☆ Does the size of the project match the amount of time the Scouts can spend working on it?

☆ What tools and materials are needed, if any, and who will provide them?

☆ Do Scout leaders have the skills to oversee the work? If not, will agency personnel be at the site to help supervise the effort?

☆ How will Scouts reach the work area?

☆ What safety factors are involved?

## After a Project

### DOCUMENTATION

Many Scout units keep logs containing reports and photographs of their conservation work. Over the months and years, these logs serve as a valuable record of Scouting's environmental activities. A log doesn't have to be fancy. In a notebook, Scouts can write down how many hours they worked and what they accomplished—feet of trail cleared, number of bird boxes installed, species and locations of trees planted, etc.—and some notes about the long-term responsibilities to maintain those projects.

Scouts who have access to a camera can also take before-and-after photographs of their work to include in their logs. With a video camera, they can film not only the results of their conservation efforts, but also much of the fun that is a part of environmental projects.

Logs, photographs, and videos are ideal for use at Scout parents' nights, courts of honor, and other gatherings that can showcase the value and excitement of Scout conservation work.

Share these records with agency resource managers, too. Documentation of completed work is very valuable for them as they assess volunteer involvement in conservation activities. Photographs and project reports can also help Scout leaders and agency personnel determine the nature and extent of future projects.

### RECOGNITION

Everyone likes to be noticed for what he or she has done. Scouting provides a variety of ways to recognize the accomplishments of Scouts involved in conservation projects. Patches, awards, and opportunities to complete requirements for merit badges and ranks are all important rewards for work well done.

Agency personnel who help Scouts undertake conservation projects also deserve recognition. They may be eligible for certain Scouting

**A logbook is a valuable record of a Scout unit's conservation activities.**

awards. A letter to an agency supervisor thanking someone for his or her help is always appreciated. Perhaps the most meaningful recognition agency personnel can receive is a sincere thank you and a handshake from Scouts in the field.

Many Scout conservation projects lend themselves to television, radio, and press coverage, especially after a Scout unit has gained some experience with environmental work. Call your local media newsrooms and alert them to upcoming projects. The stories they run may encourage other Scouts and youth groups to become involved in caring for the land.

# CHAPTER 5

# Project Leadership

As with the leadership of any aspect of Scouting, guiding Cub Scouts, Boy Scouts, and Explorers through conservation projects requires a careful balancing act. Leaders will want to do all they can to make the work go smoothly and safely, but they should never forget that the Scouts themselves are the heart and soul of environmental efforts.

In most cases, adults lead best by example. Working alongside Scouts is a much more effective motivator than watching from the sidelines as Scouts pull most of the weight.

On the other hand, a leader can sometimes do too much. Scouts should have the opportunity to take part in as many aspects of a project as possible even though adult leaders may be able to complete some work more quickly. If adults instead share their knowledge, enthusiasm, and encouragement, the benefits to Scouts and to the environment will be multiplied many times over.

Safety considerations may require that only adults do certain tasks, especially those involving power tools. Advanced planning may reveal better alternatives. For example, instead of having an adult cut logs with a chain saw, an agency may be able to provide a crosscut saw that Scouts can handle.

Varsity teams, Venture crews, and Explorer posts involved in conservation projects may be made up of both young men and young women. Leaders should see that everyone, regardless of gender, feels comfortable taking part in the work.

Invite Scouts to discuss their excitement and anxieties about using tools and attempting new kinds of work. Encourage each person to learn at his or her own speed, and to have plenty of chances to become skilled at every aspect of a project.

Make the work area a place where both males and females feel safe from ridicule and embarrassment. Discourage anyone from making fun of someone else.

## Role Models

Cub Scouts, Boy Scouts, and Explorers learn a great deal by watching adults. They are sensitive to the attitudes and actions of others and will often base their own behavior on what they see other people doing.

Conservation projects provide tremendous opportunities for Scout leaders, agency professionals, and older youth to act as effective role models. The enthusiasm they put into a project can quickly spread to others. If adults view conservation work as important, meaningful, and fun, it will probably become just as exciting to the Scouts with whom they are working.

Agency personnel who share time with Scouts will enjoy the added bonus of sharing information with young people interested in resource management careers. Scouts will look to agency personnel as sources of information and inspiration, a position most agency representatives should find very satisfying.

## Reflection

Planning an activity and doing it are important aspects of environmental explorations and of conservation projects. Of equal importance is encouraging Scouts to reflect on the experience and consider the meaning it holds for them. The process of reflection can be very informal—visiting around a campfire at the end of the day, perhaps, or talking during lunch or on the walk home.

Leaders can help Scouts think about an experience by posing questions that cannot be answered with a simple yes or no. What happened during a project? How did it feel? What did the Scouts like and not like about it? Was it similar to other adventures they've had? What impact do they think their work had on the environment? What impact did it have on them?

Scouts can also reflect on ways group members interacted with one another. Did they work well together? Did they treat each other well? Did they listen to one another? Are there ways that their group cooperation and enjoyment of future projects can be increased?

Through reflection, Scouts can better see how their actions are affecting both themselves and the land. Reflection is an opportunity to give the richest meaning to Scouting experiences.

## A Final Note on Leadership

No matter how thoroughly a leader plans Scout activities, there will be times when not much seems to go right. The weather may turn stormy, energy levels may be down, or the project may simply not be as interesting or satisfying as you had hoped.

Accept the fact that not everything will be perfect every time. This happens to every leader, Scout, and agency representative no matter how hard they try.

But also keep in mind that your perception of a project's success may be very different from that of others. Young people are resilient. They have a knack for finding excitement in almost any situation. A day full of rain, mud, and slow progress may have seemed disappointing to adults, but the Scouts may remember it as one of the great, soggy adventures of their Scouting experience.

Approach all Scouting events with enthusiasm and a willingness to make the best of any conditions. Because conservation projects have multiple objectives—fun, work, companionship, learning new skills—some of them will always be met. If you can stay cheerful and optimistic as part of your basic approach to being with young people, every conservation project will be a success.

# CHAPTER 6

# Safety

Safety is a vital consideration for every Scouting activity. Obviously, Cub Scouts enjoying a neighborhood environmental exploration will have different safety concerns than Explorers constructing a trail in rugged mountain terrain. But whatever the activity, leaders must consider the location of the project, possible weather conditions, the skill level of Scouts, and other safety aspects of both the work and the play to be done.

Address safety from the start of project planning. Scout leaders can discuss the subject with agency personnel in order to identify any hazards that should be avoided and any methods by which the safety of Scouts can be enhanced. Agencies may have their own work safety standards and will expect Scouts to follow their guidelines.

Scout leaders accompanying agency personnel on a visit to a conservation work site before a project can make a general safety assessment of the area. Does the work site seem to be generally safe, or is it too close to a cliff, a highway, or some other hazard? Will mud, smooth rock, or roots make footing difficult? Is there poison ivy or poison oak? Should Scouts be prepared for mosquitoes or ticks?

The advance visit is a good time for the agency to decide if it will close the project area to public use while Scouts are working. This precautionary measure can give Scouts more freedom to complete their tasks and will protect the public from stumbling over tools or stepping into holes. Such a closure can be especially important when the work involves trail maintenance or trail construction.

**Determine emergency procedures before they are needed.**

The visit is also an opportunity for leaders to review procedures for summoning help if an accident should occur. Where is the nearest telephone? The nearest medical facility? In the backcountry, will agency personnel be on site, and will they be equipped with two-way radios capable of contacting medical assistance?

Scouting's policy of having at least two adult leaders present during Scout activities makes it possible for one leader to take charge of a first aid emergency involving another adult. Even so, it is good practice to include Scouts in planning what to do in a medical crisis.

Emergency contact cards such as those on the next two pages contain information that should be at your fingertips if someone becomes injured or ill. Fill out the cards before a project begins. Store a Scout emergency contact card inside each group first aid kit. Give agency emergency contact cards to agency personnel.

## Emergency Telephone Numbers for Scouts

BSA council office _____

BSA after-hours contact _____

Agency headquarters _____

Agency after-hours contact _____

Rescue or emergency medical service _____

Local police or sheriff _____

Scouts and leaders who are taking part in the project:

_____

_____

_____

_____

_____

_____

_____

_____

_____

_____

_____

## Emergency Telephone Numbers for Agencies

Scout leaders who will be with the Scouts _____

_____

Scout parents who will not be at the project _____

_____

BSA council office _____

BSA after-hours contact _____

Rescue or emergency medical service _____

Local police or sheriff _____

Scouts who are taking part in the project:

_____

_____

_____

_____

_____

_____

_____

_____

## Personal Clothing and Gear

Conservation work can be dirty, dusty, muddy, and very hard on clothes. Many Scouts no doubt see that as one of the most inviting aspects of a project. Even so, they should wear clothing that affords them adequate protection and is rugged enough to withstand abuse, old enough that it doesn't matter, or both.

Clothing should be appropriate for the weather, too—warm enough for chilly or cold conditions, or cool enough for days that are hot. Cub Scouts, Boy Scouts, and Explorers who want to be in uniform may be concerned that conservation work will damage good Scout pants. The section on uniforms in the *Boy Scout Handbook* solves that problem by saying that "Scouts involved in conservation projects may wear work pants or jeans with their Scout shirts."

Keeping in mind the variable nature of weather and work, use the list below as a guide for choosing clothing and gear suitable for the conservation project at hand.

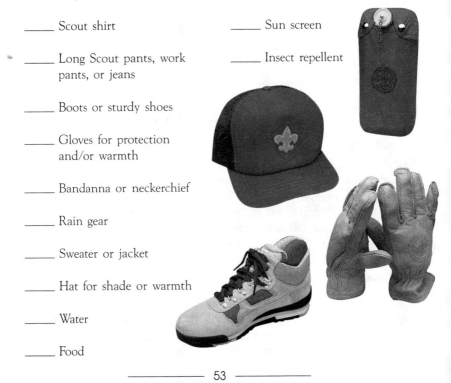

_____ Scout shirt

_____ Long Scout pants, work pants, or jeans

_____ Boots or sturdy shoes

_____ Gloves for protection and/or warmth

_____ Bandanna or neckerchief

_____ Rain gear

_____ Sweater or jacket

_____ Hat for shade or warmth

_____ Water

_____ Food

_____ Sun screen

_____ Insect repellent

A Scout unit should have at least one group first aid kit at the project site. The agency may also provide any special equipment such as hard hats that will increase Scouts' safety. The agency may require that goggles or safety glasses be worn whenever Scouts use high-impact tools such as sledgehammers or engage in activities that can cause falling dust and debris, such as trimming branches with pole saws.

## Safety Before Work

Scouts who are given a large degree of responsibility for their own protection often respond by working very safely. However, never assume they will always know what is in their best interests.

When Scouts arrive at a work site, review with them the most important safety issues relating to the upcoming project. This is a good job for a senior patrol leader, an Explorer who has helped plan the project, or the den chief of a Cub Scout den. Encourage Scouts to discuss potential hazards and ways they can ensure group safety. Outline any special safety rules and explain the reasoning behind each one. Young people are usually quite willing to follow guidelines that make sense to them. However, in the rare event that Scouts refuse to comply with basic safety standards, they should not be allowed to remain at the work site.

## Safety During Work

Scout leaders and agency personnel must set good safety examples. Scouts will be much more likely to work with care if they see adults following the same standards. Be consistent. A safety practice that is important in the morning should be followed in the afternoon, too.

While it is impossible to list every consideration that leads to safe working habits, the following practices can significantly increase the safety of project sites.

### SPACING

Scouts trained in the use of an axe know that they must maintain a safe working distance between themselves and other people—at least ten feet of free space in every direction. The ten-foot rule is a good one when using shovels, picks, and other tools, too.

**Maintain safe spacing appropriate for the task.**

## LIFTING ▲

Demonstrate correct lifting techniques for Scouts, then have them practice lifting light objects by keeping their backs straight and powering the lift with their legs.

Communication is vital on project sites. Safety is enhanced when Scouts work together as a team.

When something heavy must be moved, see that Scouts get plenty of help to make the job easier and protect themselves from injury. Encourage a teamwork approach to lifting, with plenty of clear communication both in picking up heavy objects and putting them down.

Also consider ways that lifting can be avoided. Rolling rocks and logs in a controlled manner will often move them into position with far less effort and potential danger than hoisting them off the ground.

## COMMUNICATING

Safety during conservation work is greatly enhanced if every Scout knows what the others are doing. When Scouts talk to each other with safety in mind, they are better able to stay alert, maintain proper spacing, handle tools correctly, and recognize hazardous situations.

Before the work begins, Scouts with disabilities affecting their hearing, vision, or mobility should discuss with the group how they can best convey and receive safety information.

## WEARINESS, HUNGER, AND COLD

Scouts who become tired, wet, chilled, or hungry aren't going to have much fun. They are also less likely to pay close attention to safety. A leader must be aware of the physical conditions and moods of those working on a conservation project and use common sense in adapting to changing circumstances.

If Scouts are uncomfortably damp and cold, get them into dry clothing and a shelter. If they are hungry, get them fed. And if weariness is impairing their attention level or enthusiasm, call it a day and finish the project another time. Be flexible both in planning projects and in carrying them out. It is better to stop working while Scouts are still enjoying themselves rather than pushing them beyond reasonable limits of interest, endurance, daylight, and safety.

Some units appoint a Scout as *safety officer of the day* to give special attention to the safety practices of the rest of the group. A safety officer may see hazards that others don't notice. He or she can also set a good example of safe working habits. Different Scouts can serve as safety officers on future projects.

# CHAPTER 7

# Conserving Resources

All of us consume natural resources. Our lives are made possible by the food, energy, and materials we take from our environment. We must have air to breathe and water to drink. The metal, stone, and lumber that form our buildings come from the earth, as does the fuel for our cars, trucks, ships, and aircraft. Most of the power to heat and cool our homes, run our factories, and light our cities comes from dams built across rivers, coal stripped from mines, natural gas and oil pumped out of the ground, and generators spun by nuclear reactions.

Our dependence on natural resources puts heavy burdens upon the environment. Through ignorance, greed, or lack of caring, our actions sometimes do serious harm to land, air, and water. It is crucial for the well-being of the environment that we use resources wisely—taking from our surroundings only what we need, reusing whatever we can, and repairing ecological damage and acting to prevent it from reoccurring.

Hands-on projects can help young people develop a healthy conservation ethic. Learning to live low-impact lives will enhance the futures of all of us and improve the quality of the environment both now and for generations to come.

## Partnerships in Resource Conservation

Public power companies, water districts, waste disposal systems, and other utilities encourage the conservation of resources. Many have effective educational programs that are especially designed for young people. Most also encourage people to become involved in home energy audits, precycling and recycling programs, and other efforts to reduce our reliance on natural resources.

Through environmental explorations, Cub Scouts, Boy Scouts, and Explorers can visit public utilities to learn about the reasonable use of resources. They can also become involved in programs offered by utilities to help consumers save resources, and can encourage others in their neighborhoods to become conservation-minded.

The decision to live in ways that are easy on the environment is a very personal one. As individuals or as Scout units, Scouts can begin making that choice by following easy steps to reduce the amount of resources they currently use.

## SAVING WATER

☆ Turn off water while brushing teeth.

☆ Fix dripping faucets.

☆ Install volume-control devices in showers and sinks (these are often available from public water districts).

☆ Place a water-filled plastic container in each home toilet tank to reduce the amount of water required for each flush. Flush only when necessary.

☆ Take shorter showers.

☆ Don't start a dishwasher until it is full. Use water sparingly when washing dishes by hand.

☆ For laundry, start a washing machine only when it is full of clothes, or adjust the controls to use less water for partial loads. Washing with cold water saves energy, and biodegradable soap is less harmful to the environment.

## SAVING ENERGY

☆ Turn off lights, televisions, radios, and other appliances when they are not in use.

☆ Hang wet laundry on an outdoor clothesline—a simple way to use free solar energy.

☆ Set furnace thermostats no higher than sixty-five degrees in the winter, and air-conditioning dials no lower than seventy-five degrees in the summer.

☆ Walk, bicycle, and use public transportation instead of relying on automobiles. When car travel is necessary, consider sharing rides. Plan trips ahead of time to avoid extra driving.

☆ Contact public utilities to learn about other ways Scouts and their families can make their homes more energy-efficient. Officials may suggest low-cost steps to increase insulation in attics and around water heaters, make doors and windows weather-tight, and take advantage of winter sunlight and summer shade.

## MENDING AND REPAIRING

Scouts can often repair things rather than throwing them away. Fixing broken camping gear, toys, bicycles, and other items can keep them in use for a long time. The same is true of mending worn clothes. Furniture, appliances, and clothing that are no longer needed can be donated to charitable organizations that recondition goods and recycle them in the community.

**SHOPPING SMART**

Many Scouts help with family shopping. Others have allowances they use for personal savings and purchases. Adults can act as strong role models by being discerning consumers who consider the environmental impact of their own buying practices. Encourage Scouts to think about the following ideas in making purchases:

☆ Decide ahead of time whether you really need to buy something or if what you already have will serve the same purpose.

☆ Reuse egg cartons, grocery bags, and cardboard boxes. This lessens the demand for new paper, which in turn reduces the pressure on America's forests. Many shoppers don't use store containers at all, but instead carry cloth or mesh bags that can be reused hundreds of times. A Scout day pack is a perfect shopping bag, leaving hands free for the walk home.

☆ Select products with recyclable packaging or no packaging at all. For example, fruits and vegetables that can be put into your own reusable bags are more environmentally friendly and probably less expensive than produce packed in hard-to-recycle plastic containers.

☆ Support recycling by purchasing products marked *Made from recycled materials*.

# Recycling

The average American produces more than one thousand pounds of trash a year, or nearly four pounds per day. Much of our refuse can be made into new products, turned into fuel, or used to enrich the soil. Trash that is not recycled must be dumped, usually into landfills already bulging with years of accumulated garbage.

Recycling allows consumers to use resources over and over rather than just once. Recycling also reduces energy demands. For example, twenty aluminum cans can be recycled with the same amount of energy required to make a single new can.

## WHAT SCOUTS CAN RECYCLE

National averages show that our trash contains:

41 percent paper

18 percent yard wastes

9 percent metals

8 percent glass

8 percent food waste

7 percent plastics

9 percent other

Nearly all of those materials can be recycled. For example:

**Paper**—Newspaper, computer and typing paper, paper bags, cardboard

**Glass**—Most bottles and jars

**Metals**—Aluminum cans, tin cans, foil

**Yard wastes**—Grass, leaves, shrub and tree clippings

**Plastics**—Soda bottles, milk jugs, shampoo, detergent and food containers

**Other**—Dirty motor oil and worn out batteries, clothing, appliances, furniture, and thousands of other items

## RECYCLING IN COMMUNITIES AND HOMES

☆ Scouts can set up simple recyclable collection systems in their homes. Cardboard boxes work well, one each for newspapers, mixed paper, metal cans, glass, and plastic. Wash cans, bottles, and plastic containers, and save space by flattening cans before putting them in the boxes. Find out where to take the containers when they are full (a local drop-off point or buy-back center), or whom to contact for neighborhood pickup.

☆ Yard cuttings and leaves can be composted in backyard or garden compost bins. Fruit rinds, discarded vegetables, and other non-meat food scraps can be stirred into the bins, too. The rich dirt formed by composting makes ideal potting and gardening soil.

☆ In partnership with local colleges, churches, and service organizations, Scouts may also help their communities develop good recycling habits. Many Scout units have helped establish and operate neighborhood drop-off sites where people can bring recyclables separated by type. Cooperating recycling companies can then pick up large amounts of paper, metal, glass, and plastic.

For a wealth of useful information on recycling at home, in communities, and in rural areas, contact the Environmental Protection Agency's Solid Waste Information Clearing House at 1-800-677-9424.

## Getting Involved in the Larger Picture

Many important decisions affecting our natural resources are made by local, state, and federal government agencies. As representatives of all citizens, these agencies are responsive to public concerns, but only if people make them aware of the issues that are of importance to them.

☆ Encourage Scouts to learn about environmental issues through newspapers, television and radio coverage, and on-site observations. They can watch decisions being made by visiting the offices of public officials involved with utilities, transportation, and planning, and the offices of government land management agencies.

☆ Young people can make their interests and concerns known to decision makers through letters or visits. For example, if their area does not have an active recycling program, Scouts might organize letter-writing campaigns urging local officials to explore ways that recycling can be made practical and perhaps even profitable for community.

☆ Scouts can also express their feelings to companies they believe should improve their environmental practices. In recent years, motivated customers have helped convince fast-food chains to begin using biodegradable cups, napkins, bags, and other containers. Due to consumer interest, many grocery stores now provide shoppers with reusable bags. A number of manufacturers have changed their products and packaging as a result of the public's increasing ecological awareness.

☆ Education is a valuable part of resource conservation. As they learn about the environment and ways they can protect it, Scouts can share their knowledge with other Scouts and with their communities. Here are a few of the many successful educational efforts Scouts have planned and carried out:

- *Made posters illustrating wise environmental practices, and displayed the artwork in schools and store windows.*

- *Took photographs and made videos of environmental problems, then researched solutions. Scouts presented their findings to public officials and volunteered their time to help correct troubling situations.*

- *Prepared displays of common household items that can be recycled and of new products made from recycled materials. With posters explaining how everyone can take part in recycling efforts, the displays have been used to share information at Scout meetings and community gatherings.*

# CHAPTER 8

# Trail Maintenance and Repair

Trails are among the oldest marks humans have made on the face of the Earth. They are also some of our most important recreational and environmental resources. Unfortunately, thousands of miles of American trails are endangered by overuse and by the inability of land managers to commit sufficient money and manpower to trail maintenance.

Most Scouts have walked the pathways in a city park or along a community reservoir, and many have hiked trails in Scout camps and on public lands. Scouts may know of paths where they can ride bicycles or horses, and of barrier-free trails designed for people who have special needs.

Trails provide access to lakes, rivers, mountains, and wilderness areas. They wind through forests, meadows, deserts, and urban greenbelts. Trails allow all of us to leave streets and sidewalks behind and enjoy the outdoors at a pace that is right for discovering the richness and variety of nature.

Trails also protect the environment. By providing people with a clear route of travel to reach the places they want to go, pathways limit human impact to the trails themselves, leaving the rest of the landscape untrampled. By giving people access to the outdoors, trails help them to better appreciate the environment and the importance of looking after it.

No pathway will remain in good condition unless it is maintained. Rain, snow, the impact of many footsteps, and the effects of gravity all wear out a trail. Without care, a path can become rutted and overgrown. Instead of being an environmental resource, a neglected trail may erode into an impassable scar on the land or simply fade away.

Scouts who enjoy hiking on trails can find great satisfaction in caring for the pathways they use. Worthwhile trail projects include brushing, tread maintenance, water bar installation to channel water off a trail, turnpike construction, and bridge building.

## Tools foR Trail Work

Axes and saws have long been a part of Scouting's heritage. Trail work can give Scouts opportunities to use them productively. While other trail tools may not be as familiar to Scouts, mastering them will make many conservation projects easier to accomplish.

### CARRYING TOOLS

The edges of cutting tools should be covered with sheaths whenever those tools are not in use. Carry a tool with its sharpened edge away from you. As you walk with a tool in your hand, maintain at least ten feet of space between you and other people. Hold the tool on your downhill side near your waist or thigh, *not* on your shoulder. That way, if you stumble, you can toss the tool away rather than falling with it close to your head and neck.

Keep cutting edges sharp. Be sure that handles are tight and free of splinters or splits. A tool in top condition is easier to control, and thus safer, than tools with blunted blades or loose handles.

### TOOLS FOR CUTTING

**Ax.** The *Boy Scout Handbook* details proper use and care of axes. A three-quarters ax or pack ax is a manageable tool for most young people. Axes can be used to chop deadfall from trails, shape stakes for turnpikes and water bars, and cut notches for structures made of timber.

**Bow saw.** A bow saw with a blade sixteen inches to thirty-six inches in length is handy for cutting brush and trimming branches. If a saw has no sheath, make one by splitting open a piece of old garden hose as long as the blade. Fit the hose around the saw blade and hold it in place with cord or duct tape. A sheathed bow saw can be carried by hand or strapped onto a backpack.

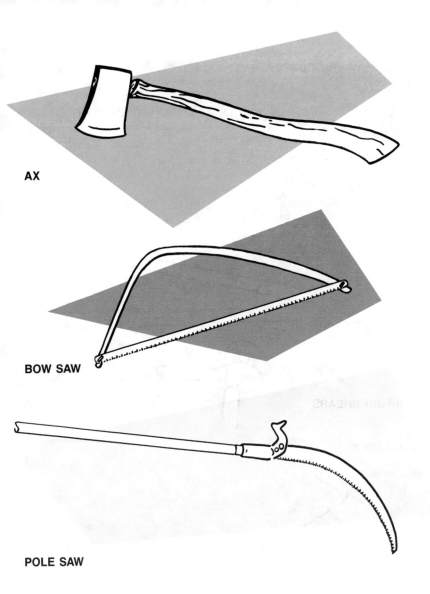

**AX**

**BOW SAW**

**POLE SAW**

**Pole saw.** A pole saw allows Scouts to trim branches more than an arm's reach above a trail. On some models, the pole can be taken apart and the blade removed for easy carrying.

**Crosscut saw.** Used a century ago by loggers felling trees, the crosscut saw is today a tool Scouts can use to cut logs for timber projects and to

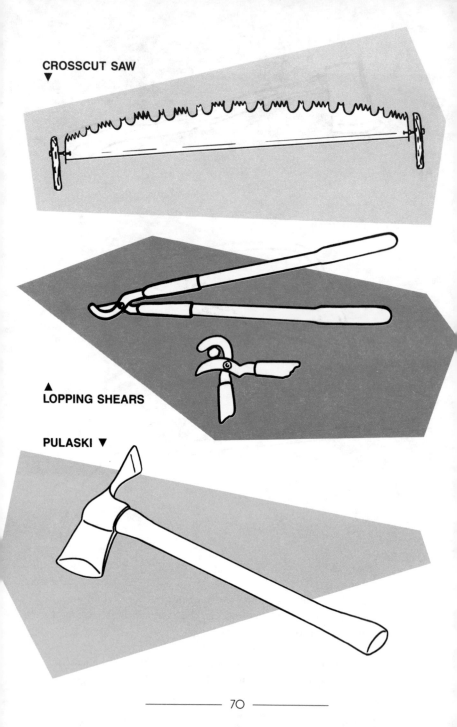

**CROSSCUT SAW** ▼

▲
**LOPPING SHEARS**

**PULASKI** ▼

clear large deadfall from trails and campsites. Two-person saws require teamwork, but with practice, Scouts can become very good sawyers. Crosscut saws must always be sheathed before they are carried very far. A sheath can be made from an old piece of fire hose. Slit the hose, fit the hose over the saw blade, and hold it in place with cord.

**Loppers.** Loppers are ideal for clearing heavy vegetation from trails. A sturdy pair will cut cleanly through all sorts of brush and branches. Carry them with the jaws pointed down and away from you, or strap them onto the back of a pack.

**Pulaski.** Named for the ranger who designed it as a tool for fighting forest fires, the Pulaski combines an ax bit with an adz-shaped hoe. With the bit and adz keenly honed, a Pulaski is a woodworking tool just right for shaping the notches and joints of turnpikes, bridges, and other timber projects. Pulaskis can also be used to loosen dirt and cut through roots, though using them that way will quickly dull the blade.

**Drawknife.** Use a drawknife to strip bark from logs for water bars, turnpikes, and other timber work. The drawknife takes its name from the manner in which woodworkers pull the tool toward themselves, the two handles providing plenty of control. A drawknife blade is *beveled*, which means that only the top of the cutting edge is sharpened. The smooth underside of the knife glides along the wood, causing the bark to curl up over the blades.

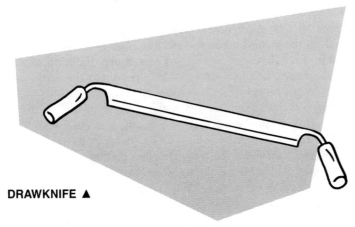

**DRAWKNIFE ▲**

**File.** Cutting tools are safer and easier to use when they are kept sharp. Sharpening them helps Scouts learn to care for the tools they use and also to master an important work skill.

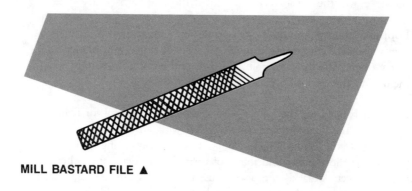

**MILL BASTARD FILE ▲**

A good all-purpose file is a *mill bastard file*, eight or ten inches long. The lines angling across the face of the file are its teeth. A sharp file will be drab gray in color. A silvery shine on a file face means many teeth have been broken or bent, and the file will not sharpen very well. Scouts sharpening tools must always protect their hands with leather gloves. The file should also have a *knuckle guard* fitted over the point, or *tang*. Guards can be made from a square of old fire hose, inner tube, or leather. Buy a file handle at a hardware store or make one from a piece of wood or a corn cob.

Brace the tool to be sharpened so that its edge is upright. An ax can be placed on the ground between a small log and two pegs or tent stakes. The adz of a Pulaski can be driven into a stump, the teeth of a McLeod (a rake-shaped forest fire tool) can be pressed into the earth, and a draw knife can be tightened into a bench vice.

Place the file on the edge of the blade and stroke it against the bit. Use enough pressure so that you feel the file cutting into the metal.

Lift the file as you draw it back for another stroke. A file sharpens only as it is pushed away from the tang. Dragging the file across the blade on the return will break off the teeth and dull the file.

Sharpen with firm, even strokes. Under bright light, a dull edge will reflect light. Continue to file until the cutting edge of the tool seems to disappear.

## TOOLS FOR DIGGING

**Shovel.** Shovels come in a variety of sizes and shapes. Agency shovels for fighting forest fires are especially useful for conservation projects. They are light in weight, sturdy, and can be sharpened to cut more easily through ground cover and soil.

**Grub hoe.** Grub hoes are good for constructing and repairing trail tread and for digging trenches to hold turnpike logs and water bars. Grub hoes are not usually sharpened.

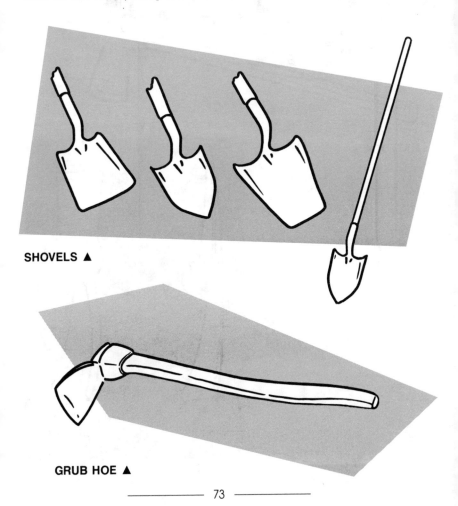

**SHOVELS ▲**

**GRUB HOE ▲**

**Mattock.** A mattock is a heavily built grubbing tool with an adz blade that can be used as a hoe for digging in hard ground. The other blade of a mattock may be a pick for prying out rocks or a cutting edge for chopping roots. As is the case with grub hoes, handles of mattocks can be removed for ease in packing.

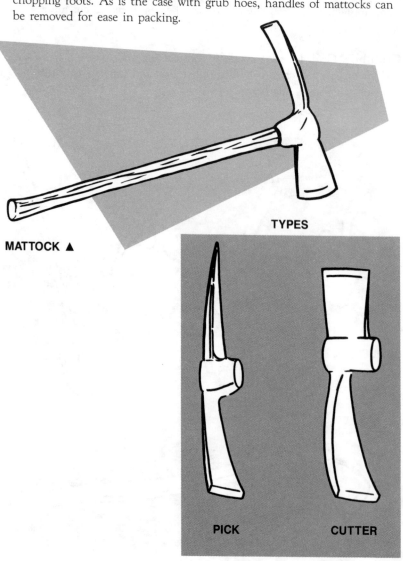

**MATTOCK ▲**

**TYPES**

**PICK**

**CUTTER**

**McLeod.** The McLeod is a forest fire tool common in America's western mountain ranges. The tines of the heavy rake are backed by a cutting edge that can be sharpened with a file. The McLeod is perfect for removing slough and berm, types of earth buildup, from a trail and smoothing tread.

The McLeod's shape makes it awkward to transport and store. Always put a sheath on the cutting edge, and carry it with the tines pointing toward the ground. At a project site or in camp, store it standing up in a spot that is out of the way.

**Garden trowel.** A trowel has dozens of uses in conservation work, from digging holes for planting tree seedings to shaping the trench for a water bar.

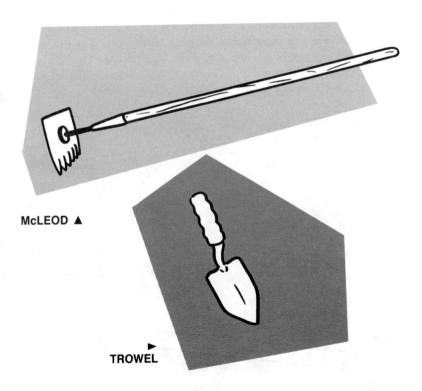

**McLEOD ▲**

▶
**TROWEL**

## TOOLS FOR ROCK

**Rock bar.** Scouts can use rock bars to move rocks they could not otherwise budge. The secret is leverage—working the beveled ends of several bars under a rock, then using smaller rocks as fulcrums to raise and ease the big stone toward its destination.

As with all hand tools, rock bars require wise use. Keep toes and fingers clear of places where they could be pinched. Work as a team, making sure everyone understands each step of a rock move before it begins.

**Sledgehammer.** A sledgehammer is very effective for crushing rock into gravel to be used in trail repair and for driving large stakes into the ground to secure water bars and turnpikes. A sledge with an eight-pound head is about the right weight for most Scouts.

Because it can cause stone chips to fly, anyone swinging a sledge-hammer must wear eye protection, long pants, and boots. Everyone else must stay out of range of bits of flying rock. When driving stakes, hit the target squarely. Striking a stake with the sledge handle rather than the hammer head may cause the handle to splinter or break.

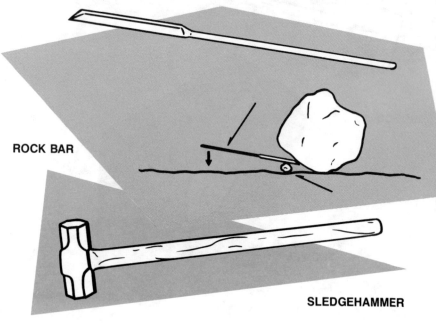

**ROCK BAR**

**SLEDGEHAMMER**

## TOOLS FOR MOVING TIMBER

**Timber carriers.** Always used in pairs, timber carriers allow four or more Scouts to share the weight of moving a log.

**Cant hook and peavy.** Steeped in the lore of the logging industry, these tools are just right for rolling log sections out of trails or for adjusting the position of logs used in timber projects. A cant hook has a spiked end while a peavy does not.

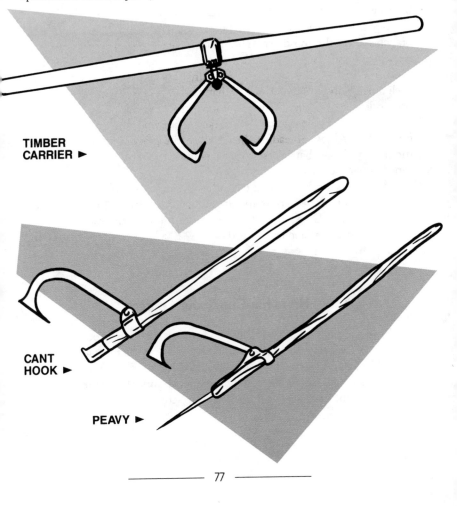

**TIMBER CARRIER ▶**

**CANT HOOK ▶**

**PEAVY ▶**

# Brushing

Vegetation encroaching upon a trail can make hiking difficult. *Brushing* involves clearing a comfortable *travelway* by cutting back tree branches and underbrush several feet on either side of the trail and about ten feet overhead.

Use loppers to clip brush close to the earth, leaving no stumps. Cut larger vegetation with bow saws, again leaving nothing protruding above the ground that could cause hikers to stumble. Trim overhead branches with pole saws.

Small tree branches can also be pruned with loppers. Remove larger branches with a bow saw by first cutting from below about a third of the way through each limb. Cut the rest of the way through the branches from the top down. The initial *undercut* will prevent a falling branch from stripping bark off a live tree.

Cut every branch flush with the trunk. That's best for the tree, and it eliminates unsightly "hat racks" that can snag passing hikers, horseback riders, pack animals, and mountain bikers.

Enhance the appearance of the trail by carrying cut branches away from the travelway. Spreading them flat on the ground will encourage the natural decay that releases nutrients into the soil to nourish new generations of plants.

If a large branch or a tree trunk has fallen across a trail, use a bow saw, a crosscut saw, or an ax to cut through it several feet on either side of the travelway. Drag or roll the freed section out of the way, then scatter wood chips or piles of sawdust.

# Hints for Cub Scout Leaders

Brushing trails is an especially good project for Cub Scouts. Most can handle loppers and bow saws, and they will see immediate results from their efforts. Set realistic goals by choosing a trail section of reasonable length. Consider combining a few hours of brushing with a picnic, a swim, or some other pack or den activity.

8'

A cleared *travelway* allows trail users ease of passage.

When pruning, prevent stripping tree bark by *undercutting* a branch before sawing it from above. Cut close to the trunk, leaving no "hat racks."

# Tread Maintenance

Experienced trail builders say that a trail's three greatest enemies are water, water, and water. Water running down a trail can scoop ruts in the *tread*—the part of a trail on which people walk. Left uncorrected, erosion may destroy a trail. On the other hand, keeping water off a trail can extend its life by many years.

The first step in repairing a damaged trail is figuring out what is harming it. For example, water eating at the tread may be flowing from a spring above the trail. Stopping future erosion could be as simple as digging a shallow channel to drain the spring water away from the trail.

Rain and melting snow can also wash soil down hillsides and deposit it on trails. A ridge of dirt that is built up along the outside edge of the tread is called a *berm*. *Slough* is soil that has fallen downhill onto the trail's inner edge. Together, they can create a narrow trough that keeps running water on the trail tread, resulting in more erosion.

Mattocks, grub hoes, and Pulaskis are good tools for loosening compacted slough and berm, while shovels and McLeods are effective for moving the soil. Use the dirt to fill ruts in the tread, or scatter it away from the trail. Packing loose soil on the edge of a trail to make it wider usually doesn't work very well. The dirt tends to slide away under the weight of hikers or horses.

A trail built across a hillside is often *outsloped*—tilted slightly so that water falling on it will run off rather than stay on the tread and cause damage. Once berm and slough have been removed, use McLeods, mattocks, and shovels to smooth trail tread with just enough outslope to ensure good drainage.


# Installing and Repairing Water Bars

Water bars channel water off a trail before it can flow down the tread and cause erosion. Trails with gentle grades may need no water bars at all or only a few to correct problem areas. Steep trails, however, may have many water bars.

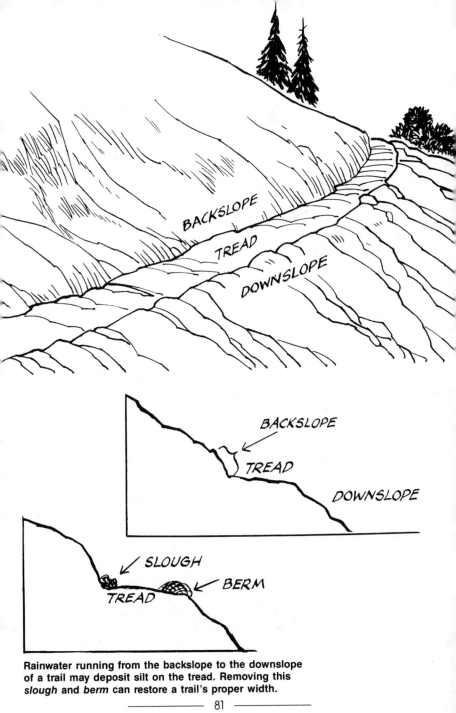

Rainwater running from the backslope to the downslope of a trail may deposit silt on the tread. Removing this *slough* and *berm* can restore a trail's proper width.

## BUILDING WATER BARS

A log for a water bar should be at least eight inches in diameter at each end and long enough to extend several feet beyond either edge of the tread. Water bars that are too small can be kicked loose by hikers and horses or washed out by rain.

Dig a trench at a forty-five-degree angle across the trail. Make its depth two-thirds that of the log's diameter. Extend the trench several feet beyond the inside edge of the trail, even if that means digging a cavity into the hillside.

Removing the bark with drawknives or axes will help keep most logs from rotting, though a few woods such as Osage orange are better left unpeeled. Place the log in the trench and pack dirt around it. Heavy wooden stakes driven into the ground on either side of the log will help hold it in place. A few stones scattered below the water bar will slow water as it leaves the trail and prevent it from eroding the hillside below.

Slope the tread as it approaches the bar so that water will curve off the trail as it nears the log. The slope of the trail should do most of the work of turning water away from the tread. The log itself serves as a barrier of last resort to stop any water that gets past the sloped area.

Water bars can also be built with rocks. Choose large stones that will fit tightly against each other in a trench angled across the trail. Place them side by side so that they form a tight wall that will divert the flow of water. Pound small gravel and dirt into the trench around the rocks to hold them in place. Test the finished water bar by standing on it, bouncing up and down. Rocks that are well chosen and properly installed will not move at all.

## MAINTAINING WATER BARS

Over time, silt can build up against a water bar. The slope of the tread that allows water to run off the trail may become beaten out of shape by hikers and erosion.

With a shovel, McLeod, or even the heel of a boot, scrape dirt from behind a water bar and pack it against the downhill side of the log or rocks. Smooth the tread as it approaches the water bar and outslope it so that the trail will again shed water.

Water bars prevent trail erosion by diverting water from the tread.

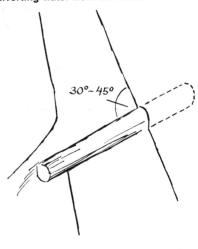

30°– 45°

## LAY WATERBAR ROCKS...
### LIKE THIS...

LOOK FOR THIS ANGLE BETWEEN THE WATER SURFACE AND THE WALKING SURFACE

NOT THIS... OR THIS.

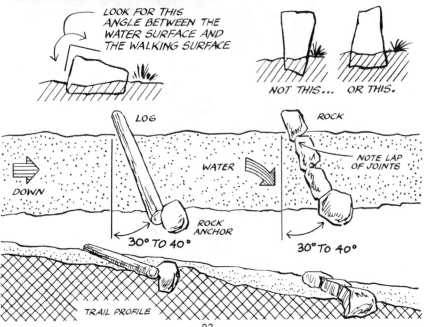

LOG

ROCK

NOTE LAP OF JOINTS

DOWN

WATER

ROCK ANCHOR

30° TO 40°

30° TO 40°

TRAIL PROFILE

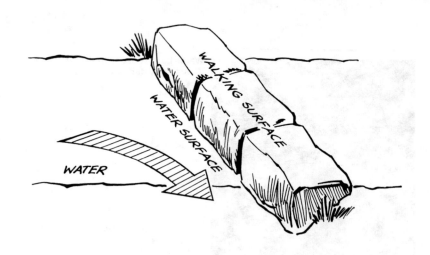

WATER

WALKING SURFACE

WATER SURFACE

**CLEANING A WATER BAR**

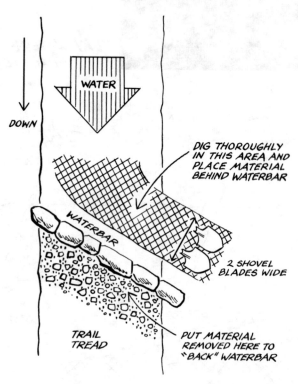

DOWN

WATER

DIG THOROUGHLY
IN THIS AREA AND
PLACE MATERIAL
BEHIND WATERBAR

WATERBAR

2 SHOVEL
BLADES WIDE

TRAIL
TREAD

PUT MATERIAL
REMOVED HERE TO
"BACK" WATERBAR

# Turnpikes

Some trails go through areas so boggy that ordinary tread cannot be kept dry. This can make it difficult for travelers who have to slog through mud. It is also hard on the land, especially if hikers, horseback riders, and mountain bikers skirting around the wet areas form ever-widening trails. One solution to a boggy trail is to build a *turnpike*.

Turnpikes are made of large rocks or logs embedded on either side of the wet trail. Stones and soil in between the rocks or logs will lift the tread above the mud. In parks and forests where regulations allow cutting, standing dead trees such as lodgepole pine are ideal sources of turnpike materials. Turnpike logs should be at least ten inches in diameter. Stripping the bark from the wood will help the logs repel water and last longer in the ground.

Dig two trenches about thirty-six inches apart and, in depth, two-thirds the diameter of the logs. Lay a log in

**The side logs of a turnpike hold rocks topped with dirt to raise the trail tread above boggy ground.**

each trench. Drive large wooden stakes into the ground along the outside of the logs to help prevent them from slipping away from the tread.

Fill the space between them with stones. Crush large stones into gravel size with sledgehammers. Spread several inches of dirt over the stones to make the tread easy on the feet of hikers and horses. Raise the center of the tread so that rain water will run off the turnpike and over the logs.

When large rocks are the building material of choice, dig trenches as you would for a log turnpike. Fit the rocks together tightly to form the sides of the turnpike, then fill in between them with stones and soil.

## Bridges

Foot bridges carry many trails over streams. Bridge construction requires both materials and expertise that may have to be supplied by a resource management agency, at least the first time Scouts undertake such a project of this magnitude. Even so, bridge building is within the abilities of many Scout units and can be an exciting and very satisfying form of trail work.

The design of a bridge depends on its location, the materials with which it is to be constructed, the snow load it must bear in the winter, and the use it will receive. Here are sketches of a few of the kinds of bridges Scouts may have the chance to help build.

**Scouts can build many kinds of footbridges.**

**PUNCHEON**

# LOG STRINGER BRIDGE

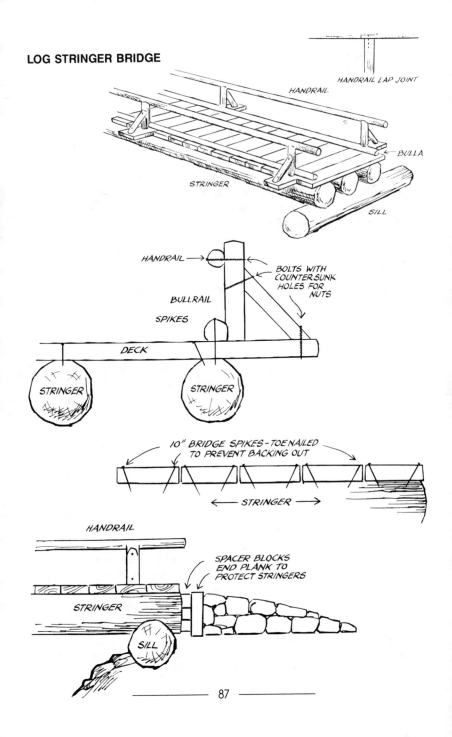

HANDRAIL LAP JOINT

HANDRAIL

BULLA

STRINGER

SILL

HANDRAIL

BOLTS WITH
COUNTERSUNK
HOLES FOR
NUTS

BULLRAIL

SPIKES

DECK

STRINGER

STRINGER

10" BRIDGE SPIKES - TOE NAILED
TO PREVENT BACKING OUT

STRINGER

HANDRAIL

SPACER BLOCKS
END PLANK TO
PROTECT STRINGERS

STRINGER

SILL

## HINTS FOR BOY SCOUT AND EXPLORER LEADERS

Trails often extend deep into parks and forests. Scout troops and Explorer posts can combine trail maintenance with backpacking trips. Each hiker can carry one hand tool. A group could either do general maintenance as they walk, or hike to a remote area in need of special attention and concentrate their efforts there.

Many parks and forests have adopt-a-trail programs that allow volunteer groups to accept responsibility for the year-round maintenance of a pathway. Such a long-term arrangement can give Scouts a deeper sense of project ownership as they regularly take care of "their" trail.

## Trail Marking

Many trails are blazed so that hikers can find their way. Long ago, blazes were often made by chopping scars into tree trunks with axes. Unfortunately, that kind of blazing injures and sometimes kills trees. Cut blazes cannot be erased if the trail route is changed.

Trail blazing today is usually done with paint. Paint poses little danger to vegetation. Various colors can be used to indicate different trail uses. If a trail is ever changed or abandoned, old marks can be eliminated by covering them with paint similar in color to tree bark.

Marking a trail and touching up existing paint blazes are suitable projects for Scouts of any age. Resource managers can determine the color and kind of paint to use and may provide brushes, buckets, scrapers or wire brushes, and materials for cleaning the tools when the work is done.

Place each blaze five or six feet above the ground on a trailside tree—higher if the trail will be used in winter where snowfall accumulates. Begin by cleaning loose bark, moss, and dirt from the tree trunk with a wire brush or scraper, taking care not to gash through the bark. Paint a rectangular blaze two or three inches wide and seven or eight inches high. Put blazes on both sides of the tree so that hikers coming from either direction will know they are on the trail.

Blazes are used mostly by travelers who are unfamiliar with an area. As a general rule, hikers standing beside one blaze should be able to look down the trail and see at least one more blaze showing them the way. Agency personnel can tell you if blazes should be closer together. They may also pick out the trees to be blazed.

## Points for Reflection on Trail Work

Trail maintenance and repair projects provide many opportunities for Scouts and adults to discuss what they are experiencing and what they are learning of the environment around them. The following issues can encourage the sharing of ideas and observations.

☆ Why are there trails? How would our use of parks and forests differ if there were no trails?

☆ How do trails protect the environment?

☆ By building a trail, humans are changing the land to serve their own needs. What other ways do we alter our surroundings? What are some of the good and bad effects of those changes?

☆ Nothing is wasted in nature. Consider how branches and brush that have been cut and scattered on the ground will decay and release nutrients for new generations of plants. How is that cycle of decay and regeneration similar to composting garbage and recycling papers?

# CHAPTER 9

# Revegetation and Restoration

Plants are some of the most visible and important signs of a healthy environment. They cleanse the air by absorbing carbon dioxide and giving off oxygen. They check erosion with leaves and branches that break the force of falling rain and root systems that hold dirt in place. Their shade slows the drying of the soil. Animals of all sorts find food and shelter among trees, grasses, and brush.

Many species of plants produce seeds and fruit we can eat. Others can be used as lumber and fuel, or turned into paper. Plants beautify our landscapes and soak up noise and pollution. In much of America, shade trees help keep houses cool in the summer, then lose their leaves and allow winter sunlight to warm our homes. Windbreaks of evergreens shield buildings from swirling winter gusts.

Explorers, Boy Scouts, and Cub Scouts can play a vital role in planting and caring for vegetation. They can also practice no-trace outdoor skills that avoid environmental damage in the first place.

## Seven Keys to No-Trace Camping

☆ Select areas appropriate for your activities.

☆ Respect agency regulations limiting the size of parties.

☆ Take along trash bags.

☆ Stow food in containers you will carry home at the end of a trip.

☆ Stay on trails.

☆ Avoid cutting across switchbacks.

☆ Select hard ground or snow for cross-country travel.

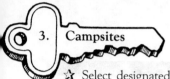

## 3. Campsites

☆ Select designated sites free of fragile plants.

☆ Camp out of sight of trails, streams, and lakes.

☆ Do not ditch tents.

## 4. Fires

☆ Build fires only when appropriate. Otherwise, use backpacking stoves.

☆ Use existing fire rings rather than making new ones.

☆ Burn small wood gathered from the ground.

☆ Make sure your fire is out.

☆ Replace sod or ground cover over burn scars.

## 5. Sanitation

☆ Dig latrines at least seventy-five steps from camps, trails, and any source of water.

☆ Use all soap and detergent at least seventy-five steps away from streams, lakes, and springs.

☆ Pour water used for washing into a sump hole.

☆ Bury sump holes and latrines and restore ground cover.

☆ Pack out all garbage and trash you have not burned.

## 6. Horses

☆ Keep number to a minimum.

☆ Tie to sturdy trees or rope.

☆ Hobble or picket animals in dry areas.

☆ Scatter manure.

## 7. Courtesy

☆ Hikers step off the trail to let horses pass.

☆ Do not pick wild flowers. Enjoy them where they are.

☆ Keep down noise around other campers and hikers. Leave radios and tape players at home.

## Window Boxes, House Plants, and Gardens

Developing a love for plants often begins in very small ways, usually through hands-on experiences. Scouts can soak beans overnight in water, then plant them in a paper cup of soil, and watch them grow. They can care for house plants and perhaps water and prune shrubs near their homes or schools. Even in the middle of a city, young people can plant flower seeds in window boxes and, in a short time, see that their efforts are making a difference in the beauty and health of a small corner of the environment.

Scouts who live in small towns and rural areas may have opportunities to plant vegetable gardens. Urban Scouts can sometimes cultivate community garden areas or transform vacant lots into "pea patch" garden plots that can be used by people living nearby.

# Tree Planting

Planting a tree encourages Scouts to take long-term responsibility for another living thing. Many trees will not reach full maturity within the lifetimes of the people who plant and care for them. Tree planting is thus an act of generosity to the present and of faith in the future. As Scouts act in the best interests of their world today, they are also improving the environment for years to come.

To be of lasting value, tree planting must be done correctly. Selecting the wrong kinds of trees, planting them in the wrong locations, or neglecting trees after they are in the ground does a disservice to the trees, the Scouts who planted them, and the people who must deal with the trees in the future. The solution, of course, is careful planning.

## GATHERING INFORMATION

Environmental explorations with nursery workers, gardeners, city officials, and foresters allow Scouts to learn why trees are important and why many areas would benefit by having more. Those experts may also suggest specific places where Scouts can plant and care for trees.

Wherever trees are to be planted, the answers to the following questions will increase the chances of success:

1. Has permission been obtained from landowners or agencies to plant on the selected site?

2. What species of trees should be planted? Are they suitable for the soil, climate, and location?

3. Is the planting site free of overhead and underground utility lines? Is city approval required before planting can take place?

4. Who will furnish the trees? Agencies may supply seedlings to be planted on public lands. Organizations, landowners, and interested businesses may be sources of funding for the purchase of young trees.

5. Planting requires shovels, buckets, water, mulch, and sometimes stakes and padded wire. Where will Scouts obtain those items? Can they be borrowed or donated?

# TREE PLANTING

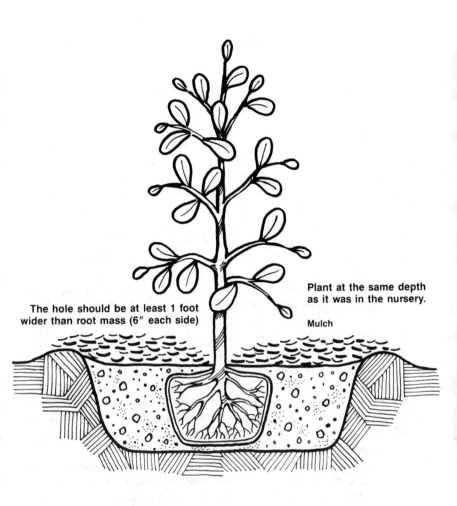

The hole should be at least 1 foot wider than root mass (6″ each side)

Plant at the same depth as it was in the nursery.

Mulch

6. Who will teach the Scouts proper planting techniques? Always involve an experienced gardener, forester, agency professional, or other knowledgeable adult to provide guidance.

7. Are Scouts willing to care for the trees after they have been planted?

8. How can Scouts get the most out of this experience? Consider ways Scouts can reflect on what tree planting means to them and to the environment around them.

## PLANTING

Trees to be planted may range in size from twelve-inch seedlings to saplings more than six feet tall. Whatever its size, a tree's roots will probably be protected by plastic or burlap, or enclosed in a bucket or box. Keep young trees in a cool, shaded location to prevent them from drying out before planting.

Dig a hole just deep enough to hold the roots and, if it has one, the ball of soil surrounding the roots. Loosen the sides and bottom of the hole so that tiny roots can more easily push into the soil.

If the tree is in a pot or other container, remove it and gently straighten any twisted roots or those growing around the root ball. Ease the tree into the hole. The crown at the top of the roots should be almost even with the surface of the ground. See that the tree is standing straight, then push loose dirt around the roots, and press it down firmly. Cover to the crown where the roots and tree trunk meet, but no deeper.

After the hole is filled, shape extra dirt into a dam encircling the tree trunk. Soak the soil with water, then soak it again. A newly planted seedling needs several gallons of water, while a larger tree can require ten gallons or more. If the tree is drooping, use stakes and padded cord or wire to give it temporary support.

Cover the ground around the base of the tree with several inches of wood chips, composted leaves, straw, grass clippings, or sawdust. This layer of *mulch* holds in moisture, enriches the soil, and discourages other plants from competing with the young tree. Spread mulch as far as the branch tips of the tree, and replenish it every year until the tree is well-established.

**FOLLOWING UP**

One of the pleasures of planting trees is enjoying their long-term care. Experts can provide Scouts with guidance on when and how to water, mulch, prune, and straighten their trees. Scouts should plant trees only if they are willing to look after them.

## REVEGETATION AND RESTORATION

Campsites, meadows, alpine zones, riverbanks, lakeshores, and other popular outdoor areas are often harmed by too much use. Heavy impact beats down vegetation. The fall of many feet compacts soil and makes it difficult for seeds to take root and grow. In short, portions of our environment are being loved to death.

Repairing damaged areas is an important conservation endeavor for Scouts. Here are three typical situations that Cub Scouts, Boy Scouts, and Explorers can help solve:

☆ Hikers scrambling to a hilltop with an expansive view have worn a steep path up a slope. Rain washing away the bare soil is turning the path into a gully.

**Once dusty and rutted from overuse, a meadow repaired by Scouts is becoming healthy and green.**

☆ A popular campsite gets so much use that the ground has become bare, dusty, and rutted. Agency personnel want to close the site so that it can heal.

☆ Backpackers staying in a meadow where there is no designated campsite have left fire rings, piles of kindling, and shallow ditches that had outlined their tents. Because the area looks used, others will be tempted to stay there, too, causing the meadow to become even more badly abused.

The first step in restoring damaged vegetation is providing people with acceptable alternatives. If hikers are not given another way to reach the top of that hill, they will probably continue to climb up the gully, flattening any revegetation work as they go. If campers are not persuaded to pitch their tents elsewhere, they will continue to use the campsites they already know about.

Decisions about alternatives will probably be made by agency personnel. Implementing those decisions can provide meaningful conservation projects for Scouts. For example, park officials might involve Scouts in constructing a new, durable trail to the top of the hill. Built to agency standards, the new trail will give hikers an inviting route to their destination without causing environmental damage. After the trail is open, Scouts can close and revegetate the gully created by the old route.

An agency eager to eliminate overused or inappropriate campsites may invite Scouts to help establish a tenting area somewhere less likely to be damaged by overuse, or may rotate the use of three or four campsites so that no single area receives unnecessary impact. Once the behavior of outdoor users has been addressed, Scouts can turn their attention to the restoration of damaged ground.

## CAMPSITE RESTORATION

Areas being restored can undergo dramatic changes. Encourage Scouts to take photographs or videos of every restoration project before, during, and after the work is completed.

Begin the closing and restoration of a campsite by scattering rocks from fire rings. If they have been blackened by fire, turn the sooty sides of stones toward the earth. Carry ashes away in buckets and scatter them over a wide area.

The heat of a campfire can sterilize the soil beneath it. With little organic matter left to support plant life, abandoned fire rings may remain barren for a very long time. Remedy the problem by borrowing rich earth from out-of-the-way spots and stirring it into the fire-damaged dirt.

The soil of heavily used areas has often been packed down by many footsteps, collapsing the tiny air pockets that seedlings and plant roots must have in order to survive. Loosening compressed soil aerates the soil and gives plants a greater chance of growing. Picks, shovels, hoes, mattocks, and Pulaskis are all effective tools for this kind of work.

In areas with sufficient rainfall and abundant vegetation close by, nature will do the rest. Otherwise, it may be necessary to sow seeds or transplant vegetation into loosened soil. The species of seeds or plants must be carefully chosen for their suitability to the area and their chances of survival.

Land managers usually try to match new vegetation with species native to the location. In many cases, plants can be dug from scattered points nearby and transplanted into a project site. Mulching with pine needles, grass clippings, or other ground cover will slow moisture loss, prevent direct sunlight from burning seedlings, and nourish new plants. Agency personnel can show Scouts the best course of action.

Take steps to discourage people from walking and camping upon a revegetation site, but try to do it without making the area unattractive. Carefully placed stones, rotting logs, and downed tree branches can effectively deter human use without detracting from the appearance of the site.

As they repair damaged terrain, Scouts should take care not to trample healthy vegetation. Soft soles such as those on running shoes are less likely to tear up plants than are the lugged soles of many hiking boots.

**Logs and rocks scattered years ago in an eroded campsite have discouraged inappropriate use and allowed vegetation to take root once again.**

# Trail Revegetation

Hikers cutting across switchbacks or leaving a trail to take shortcuts risk killing vegetation. Their thoughtless behavior can cause a scar on the land that tempts other hikers to go that way, too. The result is increasing damage to the land.

Closing an unwanted trail may involve slowing rainwater with check dams constructed of rocks or logs. Firmly embed them in the soil and make the dams wider than the trail so that water can't flow around the outside edges.

Scouts can loosen compacted trail soil using the tools and methods previously suggested for trampled campsites. Leave the trail to reseed itself naturally or transplant vegetation carefully taken from nearby locations.

Finally, scatter dead brush, logs, or stones to block the ends of the closed trail for a distance far enough to convince hikers not to go that way.

People taking shortcuts across switchbacks cause erosion by trampling plants and loosening soil. A rock barrier encourages hikers to stay on the trail.

By steering hikers onto a new trail, brush blocking an abandoned route has helped the old path heal itself and melt back into the earth. The branches will slowly rot away, too.

## REFLECTION

Encourage Scouts to imagine what an area they have repaired will look like in five, ten, twenty, and fifty years. How will water, soil, and air be improved? What animals will benefit from the vegetation, both above and below the earth's surface? If Scouts planted trees, help them think about animals that will find food and shelter in their branches, bark, and leaves. People have sometimes given trees names such as Charter Oak, Lone Pine, and the General Lee Sequoia. Scouts might want to name the trees they have planted and dedicate each one to a person or an event important in their lives.

# CHAPTER 10

# Enhancing Wildlife Habitat

Scouts who help improve a wildlife habitat are expanding their concern for the environment beyond their own interests and addressing the needs of other species. One of the many important results of enhancing animal habitats is improving the quality of the environment for all living things.

Habitat improvement is closely related to other forms of conservation. For example, improperly disposing of plastics can endanger wildlife. Bits of plastic eaten by animals mistaking them for food can cause fatal intestinal blockage or stomach ulcers. Fish and wildlife can become entangled in plastic rings discarded from six-packs of cans or bottles.

By recycling plastics and other reusable products, Scouts are protecting wildlife. Likewise, Scouting efforts to revegetate damaged land, to plant trees, and to repair eroded meadows and campsites will increase sources of food and shelter for many wild animals.

## Surveying Animal Habitats

Agencies responsible for wildlife protection need good information about conditions and changes in the areas they administer. Scouts can play an important role in conducting surveys of wildlife habitats.

Effective surveying usually requires the cooperation of agency personnel to instruct Scouts in the types of information they should gather, how the findings should be recorded, and the frequency with which the survey should be conducted. Three types of surveys are well within the skill levels of Scouts:

**Baseline surveys** establish a profile of an area to guide agencies for use in determining whether some action would be beneficial. The work may include recording kinds and numbers of animals, mapping vegetation patterns, and noting human activity.

**Monitoring surveys** done at weekly, monthly, or yearly intervals track changes occurring in an area or in particular animal or plant populations.

**Evaluation surveys** gauge the effectiveness of revegetation, habitat enhancement, and other efforts to improve and protect an area.

## Enhancing Aquatic Environments

Agency personnel can be especially enthusiastic in sharing information with Scouts about aquatic environments and suggesting what young people can do to protect those ecosystems. Most Scouts will enjoy learning about a particular river, lake, or stream near their homes. They may want to make a map tracing the route of the water from its source. Where does the water come from and where does it go? What animals live in and around the water? What conditions must exist for them to thrive? What natural and human activities have an impact on the cleanliness of the water?

Of special importance to wildlife are the *riparian zones* that border many streams and other bodies of water, and *wetlands*, including marshes, swamps, and tidal flats. Abundant moisture in these areas creates ideal growing conditions for vegetation, which attracts a rich variety of fish, birds, insects, and other wildlife.

As Scouts gain an understanding of the diversity of aquatic ecosystems, they can also examine how such environments may be threatened. Overuse, shoreline erosion, sewage, trash, and toxic wastes can all degrade the quality of water, damage habitat, and endanger the animals living there.

### MARKING STORM DRAINS

Storm drains are designed to channel rainwater away from city streets and carry it to rivers or lakes. Unfortunately, some people also use the drains for getting rid of gasoline, dirty motor oil, and chemicals. Those toxic wastes flow into open water where they can seriously harm wildlife habitats.

In cooperation with city street and water departments, Scouts can perform an important community service by painting a warning slogan on the pavement near each drain:

# DUMP NO WASTE
# DRAINS TO STREAM

City officials may provide stencils, spray paint, and guidance on cleaning the pavement before painting, aligning the slogan, and completing a good job. Scouts can follow up their work by distributing informational fliers throughout each neighborhood to explain why wastes should not be dumped into storm drains and to suggest places people can take waste products for recycling or proper disposal.

## CLEANING UP STREAMS

Many lakes and streams suffer from trash dumped directly into them or washed in by storms. Cleaning up the litter can greatly improve the appearance of an area and make it much more inviting for fish and other wildlife.

**Young people working in and around water must be especially aware of their own safety and that of others.**

The involvement of resource managers increases the ease and efficiency of most clean-up efforts. As Scouts plan a project, they learn how best to get trash out of the water and what to do with it once it is ashore. They may also discover that they should leave in place some downed trees, old tires, and other objects that are slowing the current, stabilizing the streambed, or providing shelter for fish.

## INCREASING FISH POPULATIONS

Scout units near public lands may have the chance to assist agency personnel in raising fish in hatcheries and releasing them in lakes and streams. Scouts can sometimes help construct water breaks in streams to provide fish with quiet water or build and maintain spawning and foraging areas for stocked and native species. In some parts of the country, Scout units collect discarded Christmas trees, attach weights to them, and sink them in ponds where they create ideal shelter for many species of fish.

## Working Safely in Streams and Lakes

Scouts participating in any projects around water must observe special safety practices:

☆ Never work alone. The buddy system used by Scout units during swimming activities is an important safety precaution whenever young people are around water.

☆ Wear rubber boots, waders, or shoes to provide sure footing and protect feet from sharp objects.

☆ Stay out of moving water that is more than knee deep.

☆ Bring dry clothing to put on after work or if Scouts become chilled.

☆ Wash exposed skin with clean water and soap immediately after a project.

## Caring for Birds

Wherever they live, Scouts can enhance the habitats of bird populations near their homes and on public lands. Constructing and placing birdhouses and feeders allows Scouts to practice carpentry, project design, and wildlife study. They can also keep records of the birds they see, their nesting habits, and the vegetation and food each species prefers.

### BIRDHOUSES

Many species of birds seek out the hollows of trees as locations for their homes. Birdhouses increase the number of sites where birds are likely to nest. Well-made birdhouses will also protect eggs and chicks from the elements and from predators.

Local bird enthusiasts and agency personnel can guide Scouts in choosing birdhouse designs appropriate for birds of your area. The following design is easy to build and inviting to many species of birds.

You'll need a ¾-inch board that's 6½ inches wide and 5 feet long. Or, use pieces of scrap wood.

Late winter and early spring are the best times to put up birdhouses. Mounted on fence posts or trees, they should be oriented so that their entry holes face away from prevailing winds which would blow rainwater inside. After each nesting season, remove the top and clean the interior to get it ready for the next year's birds.

## BIRD FEEDERS

Feeding birds gives Scouts an enjoyable way to observe the habits of wild animals and to gain an understanding of their needs. A simple feeder on a windowsill or a feeder hung from a tree or the eaves of a roof can attract many kinds of birds. Keep feeders filled during hard winters so that birds accustomed to finding food there will always have enough to eat.

## VEGETATION

Birds are attracted to vegetation that supplies them with food and shelter. Scouts may enhance an area by planting trees and shrubs that produce seeds, nuts, and fruit for birds and other wildlife. Allowing a portion of a grassy area to grow without mowing will further increase food sources and provide birds with nesting materials.

1. Mark off the box parts with a pencil, tape measure, and carpenter's square. (Hint: measure the three straight edges on each side piece first, and the angled edge will automatically be correct.)

2. Cut out the pieces. Saw off the corners of the bottom piece to assure good drainage and airflow in the birdhouse.

3. Drill a 1½-inch entrance hole 2 inches below the top edge of the front piece.

4. Nail together the sides, bottom, and front pieces with small nails. Center this three-sided box on the back piece. About 3 inches of the back piece will extend above and below the nest box.

5. Place the top piece on the box. Position a 1-inch-by-1½-inch-by-5½-inch strip above the top piece and mark its position on the back board with a pencil.

Remove the top and lay the box on its back. Spread wood glue on the back of the strip and stick it to the back board. Nail the strip in place with several small nails. The top will fit snugly under the strip. Secure it with a washer and wood screw that goes through the top piece and into the top edge of the front.

6. If you paint the birdhouse, use nontoxic paint free of creosote or lead that could harm birds. Never paint the inside of a birdhouse or the edges of the entrance hole.

# BIRDHOUSE

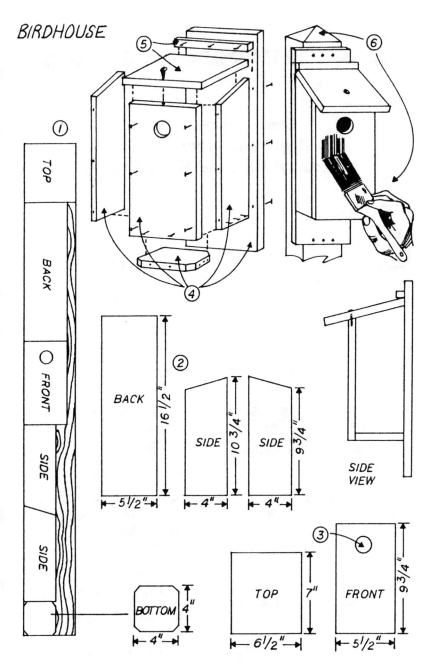

TOP
BACK
FRONT
SIDE
SIDE
BOTTOM

BACK — 16 1/2" — 5 1/2"

SIDE — 10 3/4" — 4"

SIDE — 9 3/4" — 4"

SIDE VIEW

BOTTOM — 4" — 4"

TOP — 7" — 6 1/2"

FRONT — 9 3/4" — 5 1/2"

![ ](gray bar)

# Conservation-Related Requirements for Ranks, Arrow Points, and Merit Badges

Every Scout has many opportunities to learn about the environment and complete important conservation projects. This appendix highlights the environmentally oriented requirements for various Cub Scout, Boy Scout, and Explorer ranks and lists merit badges, Arrow Point electives, and activity badges that have a conservation focus.

## Cub Scout Requirements

### WOLF CUB SCOUT ACHIEVEMENTS

5. Tools for Fixing and Building

   5e. Use a pattern or a plan to make a birdhouse, a set of bookends, or something else useful.

6. Start a Collection

   6a. Make a collection of anything you like. Start with ten things. Put them together in a neat way.

   6b. Show and explain your collection to another person.

7. Your Living World

   7a. Pick up litter you see. Put it where it belongs. Or recycle it.

   7b. List ten ways your neighborhood gets dirty. Don't forget the air and water.

   7c. Write three ways to make where you live more beautiful. Then do them.

7d. With a grown-up, find three or four stories from newspapers or magazines that tell how people are protecting our living world. Read and discuss them together.

7e. Energy is a resource. List three ways you can save energy. Save energy by doing them.

10. Family Fun

10b. Plan a walk. Go to a park or a wooded area, or visit a zoo or museum with your family.

## WOLF CUB SCOUT ARROW POINT ELECTIVES

13. Birds

a. Make a list of all the birds you saw in a week and tell where you saw them (field, forest, marsh, yard, or park).

b. Put out nesting material (yarn and string) for birds and tell which birds might use it.

c. Read a book about birds.

d. Point out ten different kinds of birds (five may be from pictures).

15. Grow Something

a. Plant and raise a box garden.

b. Plant and raise a flower bed.

c. Grow a plant indoors.

d. Plant and raise vegetables.

## BEAR CUB SCOUT ACHIEVEMENTS

5. Sharing Your World with Wildlife

5a. Choose a bird or animal that you like and find out how it lives. Make a poster showing what you have learned.

5b. Build or make a bird feeder or birdhouse.

5c. Explain what a wildlife conservation officer does.

5d. Visit one of the following: zoo, nature center, wildlife refuge, game preserve.

5e. Name one animal that has become extinct in the past hundred years. Tell why animals become extinct.

6. Take Care of Your Planet

   6a. Save five pounds of glass or aluminum, or one month of newspapers, and turn in at a recycling center.

   6b. Plant a tree in your yard, or on the grounds of the group that operates your Cub Scout pack, or in a park. Be sure to get permission first.

   6c. Call city or county officials or your trash hauling company and find out what happens to your trash after it is hauled away.

   6d. Do a water-usage survey in your home. Note all the ways water is used. Look for any dripping faucets.

   6e. Discuss with one of your parents the ways your family uses energy.

   6f. Find out more about your family's use of electricity.

## BEAR CUB SCOUT ARROW POINTS

2. Weather

12. Nature crafts

14. Landscaping

15. Water and soil conservation

## WEBELOS ACTIVITY BADGES

Forester

Geologist

Naturalist

# Boy Scout Ranks

## SECOND CLASS

2a. Since joining, have participated in five separate troop/patrol activities (other than troop/patrol meetings), two of which included camping overnight.

2b. On one campout, demonstrate proper care, sharpening, and use of knife, saw, and ax.

4. Participate in an approved (minimum of one hour) service project.

5. Identify or show evidence of at least ten kinds of wild animals (birds, mammals, reptile, fish, mollusks) found in your community.

**FIRST CLASS**

3. Since joining, have participated in ten separate troop/patrol activities (other than troop/patrol meetings), three of which included camping overnight.

6. Identify or show evidence of at least ten kinds of native plants found in your community.

7a. Demonstrate tying the timber hitch and clove hitch and their use in square, shear, and diagonal lashings by joining two or more poles or staves together.

8a. Demonstrate tying the bowline (rescue) knot and how it's used in rescues.

**STAR**

4. While a First Class Scout, take part in service projects totaling at least six hours of work. These projects must be approved by your Scoutmaster.

**LIFE**

4. While a Star Scout, take part in service projects totaling at least six hours of work. These projects must be approved by your Scoutmaster.

**EAGLE**

5. While a Life Scout, plan, develop, and give leadership to others in a service project helpful to any religious institution, any school, or your community. The project must be approved by your Scoutmaster and troop committee and approved by the council or district before you start.

## MERIT BADGES

The BSA merit badge program for Boy Scouts provides young people with dozens of opportunities to master new skills, investigate careers, and learn about the world around them. Many merit badges are closely related to conservation projects and environmental concerns. Three of those are among the twenty-one badges a Boy Scout must earn in order to receive the Eagle Scout Award.

**Environmental Science.** Currently the third most-earned merit badge behind Camping and Swimming, the Environmental Science badge helps Scouts better understand the world around them. The requirements encourage a combination of environmental observations and hands-on projects for learning about and improving the environment.

**Citizenship in the Community.** Requirements 6, 7, 8, and 10 allow Scouts to explore the roles of agencies and individuals to provide services and improve conditions in all aspects of a community including the care of the environment.

**Citizenship in the Nation.** Requirement 6 helps Scouts recognize important functions of national government. Among those areas a Scout may wish to learn about are the federal government's efforts to manage public lands.

## MERIT BADGES THAT INCREASE ENVIRONMENTAL AWARENESS

Many merit badges invite Scouts to develop a greater understanding and appreciation of ecosystems, of the complexity of nature, and of the effects of human actions upon the environment. They include:

| | | |
|---|---|---|
| Beekeeping | Energy | Forestry |
| Bird Study | Fish and Wildlife Management | Gardening |
| Botany | | General Science |
| | Fishing | |
| Chemistry | | Geology |

| Insect Study | Oceanography | Reptile Study |
| Journalism | Photography | Soil and Water Conservation |
| Landscape Architecture | Plant Science | Veterinary Science |
| Mammal Study | Public Health | Weather |
| Nature | Pulp and Paper | |

## MERIT BADGES INVOLVING OUTDOOR LIVING AND THE ENVIRONMENT

These merit badges encourage Scouts to enjoy the outdoors in ways that cause no damage to the environment. The knowledge they gain can also help them travel to sites of conservation projects, to camp near them while completing environmental work, and to carry out the tasks themselves:

| Backpacking | Cooking | Hiking |
| Camping | Cycling | Rowing |
| Canoeing | | |

## MERIT BADGES INVOLVING INFORMATION AND THE ENVIRONMENT

Some merit badges ask Scouts to produce information that is written, filmed, drawn, or spoken, or to read books. In each case, Scouts can select environmental issues as the subjects of the literary, video, and artistic endeavors required to earn these badges:

| Cinematography | Graphic Arts | Public Speaking |
| Communications | Journalism | Reading |

## MERIT BADGES INVOLVING WORK SKILLS AND THE ENVIRONMENT

From fixing leaking faucets to building structures that enhance wildlife habitat and designing rustic bridges, the hands-on work of conservation requires many skills. Merit badge requirements asking Scouts to complete certain kinds of projects can often be fulfilled with work that is oriented toward conservation. Each of the following badges increases Scouts' abilities to repair and improve their environment:

| | | | |
|---|---|---|---|
| Masonry | Model Design and Building | Pioneering | Surveying |
| Metalwork | Painting | Plumbing | Woodwork |

## Conservation Requirements for Other Scout Awards

### FIFTY-MILER AWARD

The Fifty-Miler Award recognizes Scouts who complete lengthy wilderness trips. In addition to planning and completing such an adventure, Scouts interested in earning the award must do the following:

3. During the time on the trail or waterway, complete a minimum of ten hours each of group work on projects to improve the trail, springs, campsite, portage, or wilderness area. If, after checking with recognized authorities, it is not possible to complete ten hours each of group work on the trail, a similar project may be done in the unit's home area. (There should be no unauthorized cutting of brush or timber.)

### PAUL BUNYAN WOODSMAN

This patch is given to Scouts who have proven their skill with a saw and ax. Requirement 4 encourages Scouts to use that skill for the good of the environment:

4. With official approval and supervision, do **one** of the following: (a) Clear trails or fire lanes for two hours. (d) Build a natural retaining wall or irrigation way to aid in a planned conservation effort. (e) Participate in a conservation effort project in your council.

# Resource Management Agencies and Nonprofit Conservation Organizations

## Federal Agencies

Most public lands are managed by one or more agencies. Many agencies have programs that involve volunteers in the care and protection of natural resources. You can learn about those programs and other conservation opportunities by calling, writing, or visiting agency offices. Look in your telephone book for local numbers and addresses.

The agencies administering the greatest expanses of public lands are those of the federal government. They include the following:

### U.S. Forest Service (USFS)
U.S. Forest Service
Department of Agriculture
P.O. Box 96090
Washington, DC 20013-6090

The U.S. Forest Service manages nearly 200 million acres of America's forests and rangelands, including 156 national forests, 83 experimental forests and ranges, 19 grasslands, and 16 land utilization projects. USFS also conducts research to find better ways to manage and use our national resources and helps private landowners adopt good forest practices.

Gifford Pinchot, the agency's first chief, stated the guiding principle of national forest management as "the greatest good to the greatest number in the long run." National forests serve many public interests including harvesting resources and developing recreational opportunities. Parts of some forests are set aside as wilderness areas to preserve the unspoiled quality of the environment.

The USFS is divided into six *regions* serving the various parts of the country. Each regional office oversees the activities on its *forests*, which are further divided into *districts* directed by district rangers. Scouts are most likely to work with USFS personnel at the district level.

## Soil Conservation Service (SCS)
Soil Conservation Service
U.S. Department of Agriculture
P.O. Box 2890
Washington, DC 20013

The Soil Conservation Service provides technical and educational assistance to help the public with watershed projects, flood protection, water supply management, and the improvement of recreational areas and wildlife habitat. BSA council staff often turn to this agency for guidance on how best to care for the natural resources of Scout camps.

## National Park Service (NPS)
National Park Service
U.S. Department of Interior
P.O. Box 37127
Washington, DC 20013-7127

Established in 1916, the National Park Service is directed by Congress ". . . to promote and regulate the use of the national parks, monuments, and reservations . . . to conserve the scenery and the natural and historic objects and the wildlife therein . . . by such means as will leave them unimpaired for the enjoyment of future generations."

The NPS administers 337 areas that include 79 million acres of our natural, historical, and cultural heritage. National parks, national recreation areas, national monuments, or national seashores can be found in almost every state in the Union, as well as Guam, Puerto Rico, and the Virgin Islands.

In addition to protecting natural resources, the NPS strives to provide the public with excellent opportunities for camping, backcountry exploration, hiking, horseback riding, swimming, boating, cross-country skiing, and the study of nature and American history. Volunteers are encouraged to become involved in appropriate park care and management efforts.

### Bureau of Land Management (BLM)
Bureau of Land Management
U.S. Department of Interior
Eighteenth and C Streets, NW, Room 5600
Washington, DC 20240

The jurisdictions of the Bureau of Land Management contain rugged desert landscapes, evergreen forests, snowcapped mountains, and an abundance of wildlife. Covering more than 272 million acres—almost half of all federally owned lands—BLM areas are managed under multiple-use principles that include outdoor recreation, fish and wildlife production, livestock grazing, timber harvesting, industrial development, watershed protection, and onshore mineral production.

Outdoor recreation is allowed in most BLM areas. In cooperation with BLM personnel, Scout units and other youth groups have completed significant work enhancing waterways, trails, and camping areas.

### U.S. Fish and Wildlife Service (FWS)
Assistant Director for Fish and Wildlife
Enhancement, FWS
U.S. Department of Interior
Eighteenth and C Streets, NW, Room 3020
Washington DC 20240

The mission of the U.S. Fish and Wildlife Service is to conserve, protect and enhance fish, wildlife, and their habitats for the benefit of the American people. It is dedicated to the preservation of all wildlife. Its primary responsibilities are for migratory birds, endangered species, freshwater and migratory fisheries, and certain marine mammals. From the Arctic Ocean to the South Pacific, and from Maine to the Caribbean, the FWS manages nearly five hundred national wildlife refuges. Varying in size from half-acre parcels to thousands of square miles, the refuges encompass more than ninety million acres of the nation's wildlife habitats. These areas make up the world's largest and most diverse collection of lands set aside specifically for wild animals.

The FWS also sets migratory bird-hunting regulations, leads efforts to restore endangered animals and plants, and administers a nationwide network of law enforcement agents. Volunteers have been of great help to the FWS in enhancing wildlife habitat, monitoring animal activity, and conducting important biological studies.

### Bureau of Reclamation
Public Affairs Office, BLM
U.S. Department of Interior
1849 C Street, NW, Mail Stop 7644
Washington DC 20240

The Bureau of Reclamation was created in 1902 to reclaim arid lands in seventeen western states. Projects of the Bureau of Reclamation provide water to more than ten million acres of land. In addition, reclamation efforts provide municipal and industrial water, hydroelectric power, recreational opportunities, and fish and wildlife enhancement.

### U.S. Army Corps of Engineers
Office of Public Affairs
U.S. Army Corps of Engineers
200 Massachusetts Avenue, NW
Washington, DC 20314

The Corps of Engineers in the Department of the U.S. Army was established to serve construction needs of America's military forces. The Corps of Engineers has also built many of America's harbors and waterways. Reservoirs behind dams constructed by the Corps of Engineers are recreational retreats for many Americans.

The Corps of Engineers strives to maintain and create conditions under which the human and natural environments can exist in productive harmony. Projects are also designed with the intent of preserving important historic and archeological resources. Scout groups can often undertake conservation work that improves the shorelines, trails, and campgrounds under the management of the Corps of Engineers.

## Environmental Protection Agency (EPA)
Environmental Protection Agency
401 M Street, SW
Washington, DC 20460

The Environmental Protection Agency implements federal laws designed to protect the environment. Established in 1970 as an independent agency in the executive branch of the federal government, the EPA helps Americans maintain clean air, water, and land, and prevent pollution that can cause future damage to the environment.

The EPA works to protect every aspect of our nation's environment by aggressively pursuing source reduction and recycling as an integral part of all its mandated regulation and control activities. One of its goals is the reduction of household hazardous waste through state and local recycling programs.

EPA personnel are valuable sources of information for volunteers interested in developing workable recycling programs in their neighborhoods and for those seeking active ways to become involved in cleaning up their community's air, land, and water.

## STATE, COUNTY, AND CITY AGENCIES

States, counties, and cities all have agencies dedicated to the management, preservation, and maintenance of the natural resources within their jurisdictions. Their names indicate the scope of their responsibilities—for example, departments of ecology, state parks departments, county forestry commissions, game management agencies, departments of natural resources, and city offices of parks and recreation.

Many of these agencies can involve youth groups in conservation projects on public lands. Others will provide guidance for Scouts interested in recycling programs and related efforts that enhance communities. Leaders can find addresses and numbers of agencies in telephone directories.

# NONPROFIT CONSERVATION ORGANIZATIONS

Many non-profit organizations encourage volunteers to undertake conservation projects. Some direct their efforts toward a particular type of work such as trail maintenance or the improvement of wildlife habitat, or concentrate their activities in certain geographic areas. Other organizations, including the Boy Scouts of America, are more general in their approach and national in their focus.

The organizations described in this section represent a sampling of a very large network of conservation-oriented groups interested in helping young people learn to care for the environment. Many can provide Scout leaders with information about their programs, as well as guidance for involving Scout units in conservation projects.

## American Hiking Society
1015 Thirty-First Street, NW
Washington, DC 20007
703-385-3252

American Hiking Society promotes the interests of hikers and helps preserve the trails on which they walk. Through work trips and a yearly directory of volunteer opportunities on public lands entitled *Helping Out in the Outdoors*, the organization encourages hikers to become involved in trail construction and maintenance and offers trail users facts on protecting the environment while hiking and camping.

## American Trails
1400 Sixteenth Street, NW
Washington, DC 20036
202-483-5611

American Trails promotes the planning, development, and maintenance of trails systems on public and private lands. Composed of trail clubs, agencies, individuals, and landowners, it compiles and distributes information about trails and the issues affecting them.

## Appalachian Mountain Club

5 Joy Street
Boston, MA 02108
617-523-0636

The Appalachian Mountaiins Club enjoys a long legacy of service to the backcountry of America's northeastern states. Members take part in conservation work, including trail and shelter maintenance, preservation, research, and outdoor education. The AMC's guidebooks, maps, educational programs, and service opportunities serve as valuable resources for leaders of many youth organizations.

## Appalachian Trail Conference

P.O. Box 807
Harpers Ferry, WV 25425
304-535-6331

The Appalachian Trail is one of America's great recreational treasures. Wandering 2,100 mountainous miles from central Maine to northern Georgia, most of the trail was built by volunteers.

Today, volunteers clear the trail of brush, maintain the tread, and repair campsites and shelters. Many Scout troops and Explorer posts have found great satisfaction in caring for sections of the trail.

The Appalachian Trail Conference distributes materials of importance to those wishing to hike portions of the trail and to those eager to help maintain it. The thirty-two hiking clubs that make up the conference encourage Scout groups and other volunteers to join them for ongoing conservation projects along the Appalachian Trail and other footpaths in the eastern states.

## Izaak Walton League of America

1401 Wilson Boulevard, Level B
Arlington, VA 22029
703-528-1818

Formed in 1922, the league promotes protection and preservation of natural resources, encourages conservation education, and defends America's soil, air, woods, waters, and wildlife. Some Izaak Walton chapters are chartered to operate Scouting units. All chapters can provide valuable resource information about local environmental issues and conservation projects. The league's Save Our Streams (SOS) program encourages participants to adopt a stream by conducting water and habitat quality monitoring and completing appropriate restoration activities.

## National Arbor Day Foundation
100 Arbor Avenue
Nebraska City, NE 68410
402-474-5655

The National Arbor Day Foundation encourages the planting of trees through educational programs including Trees for America, Arbor Day, Tree City USA, and Conservation Trees. The publications offered by the foundation can be of help to youth group leaders interested in making tree planting part of their programs.

## Rails to Trails Conservancy
1400 Sixteenth Street, NW, Suite 300
Washington, DC 20046
202-797-5400

The Rails to Trails Conservancy cooperates with local recreation and conservation organizations to convert abandoned railroad corridors into recreational trails. While much of the conservancy's work involves land acquisition, the organization also encourages volunteers to help with the construction and maintenance of travelways.

## Sierra Club
730 Polk Street
San Francisco, CA 94109
415-776-2211

Founded by naturalist John Muir to help everyone explore, enjoy, and protect the wild places of Earth, the Sierra Club promotes responsible use of Earth's ecosystems and resources, and enlists people in the protection and restoration of the environment. Sierra Club service trips combine backcountry living with opportunities for volunteers to restore trails and repair damaged campsites.

## Student Conservation Association
P.O. Box 550
Charlestown, NH 03603
603-826-4301

The SCA High School Program gives students ages sixteen to eighteen expenses-paid opportunities to live for a month or more in small groups completing exciting conservation projects in the backcountry of parks and forests across America. The SCA Resource Assistant Program places volunteers age eighteen and over in twelve-week internships with natural resource agencies. The SCA Wilderness Work Skills Program offers training in trail work, revegetation, and traditional and contemporary land management skills to Scout leaders, agency professionals, conservation corps members, and others.

## TreePeople
2601 Mulholland Drive
Beverly Hills, CA 90210
818-753-4600

By teaching individuals and groups how to plant and maintain trees, TreePeople emphasizes the importance of diverse groups working together for the common good. The organization also encourages young people to recognize the power they have to improve the environment.

## Regional Nonprofit
## Conservation Organizations

**Adirondack Mountain Club**
Rural Route 3, Box 3055
Lake George, NY 12845

**Akron Metro Parks Hiking Club**
3415 Twenty-First Street, NW
Canton, OH 44708

**Allentown Hiking Club**
431 Ridge Valley Road
Sellersville, PA 18960

**Appalachian Long Distance Hikers**
13220 Yates Ford Road
Clifton, VA 22024

**Batona Hiking Club**
8014 Cooke Road
Philadelphia, PA 19117

**Benton McKay Trail Association**
P.O. Box 53271
Atlanta, GA 30305

**Berkeley Hiking Club**
P.O. Box 147
Berkeley, CA 94701

**Blue Mountain Eagle Climb Club**
P.O. Box 3523
Reading, PA 19605

**Buckeye Trail Association**
4406 Maplecrest Avenue
Parma, OH 44134

**The Cascadians**
P.O. Box 2201
Yakima, WA 98907

**C and O Canal Association**
P.O. Box 366
Glen Echo, MD 20812

**Capitol Hiking Club**
3324 Glenmore Drive
Falls Church, VA 22041

**Carolina Mountain Club**
P.O. Box 68
Asheville, NC 28802

**Center Hiking Club**
4608 Coachway Drive
Rockville, MD 20852

**Central Arizona Backpackers Association**
5 South Pueblo Street
Gilbert, AZ 85234

**Chatham Trails Association**
36 Galloway Road
Chelmsford, MA 01824

**Chemeketans**
P.O. Box 864
Salem, OR 97308

**Chinook Trail Association**
P.O. Box 997
Vancouver, WA 98666

**Cleveland Hiking Club**
2508 Portman Avenue
Cleveland, OH 44109

**Coastal Conservancy**
1330 Broadway
Suite 1100
Oakland, CA 94612

**Colorado Mountain Club**
2530 West Alameda Avenue
Denver, CO 80219

**Continental Divide Trail Society**
P.O. Box 30002
Bethesda, MD 20814

**Contra Costa Hills Club**
c/o YWCA
1515 Webster, Suite 434
Oakland, CA 94612

**Cuyahoga Trails Council**
1607 Delia Avenue
Akron, OH 44320

**Dartmouth Outing Club**
P.O. Box 9
Hanover, NH 03755

**Desert Trail Association**
P.O. Box 589
Burns, OR 97720

**Diablo Hiking Club**
3424 Sentinel
Martinez, CA 94553

**Finger Lakes Trail Conference**
P.O. Box 18048
Rochester, NY 14618

**Florida Trail Association**
P.O. Box 13708
Gainesville, FL 32604

**Foothills Trail Club**
13781 Fish Hill Road
South Wales, NY 14129

**Foothills Trail Conference**
P.O. Box 3041
Greenville, SC 29602

**Genesee Valley Hiking Club**
94 Sunset Trail, West
Fairport, NY 14450

**Georgia Appalachian Trail Club**
P.O. Box 654
Atlanta, GA 30301

**Greeneville Hiking Club**
Route 3, Box 274
Chuckey, TN 37641

**Green Mountain Club**
P.O. Box 889
Montpelier, VT 05602

**Green Valley Hiking Club**
2481 South Avenida Loma Linda
Green Valley, AZ 85614

**Hayward Hiking Club**
18573 Reamer Road
Castro Valley, CA 94546

**Hood Hiking Club**
Hood Junior High School
Derry, NH 03038

**Huachuca Hiking Club**
3705 Shawnee Drive
Sierra Vista, AZ 85635

**Iowa Natural Heritage Foundation**
444 Insurance Exchange Building
Des Moines, IA 50309

**Iowa Trails Council**
1201 Central
Center Point, IA 52213

**Kanawha Trail Club**
P.O. Box 4474
Charleston, WV 25364

**Keystone Trails Association**
1113 Center Lane
State College, PA 16801

**La Canada Flint Ridge Trail Council**
P.O. Box 852
La Canada-Flint, CA 91012

**Lancaster Hiking Club**
P.O. Box 6037
Lancaster, PA 17603

**Maine Appalachian Trail Club**
P.O. Box 283
Augusta, ME 04330

**Michigan Trailfinders Club**
2680 Rockhill, NE
Grand Rapids, MI 49505

**Midstate Trail Committee**
21 Radmore Road
Worchester, MA 01602

**Minnesota Rovers Outing Club**
P.O. Box 14133
Minneapolis, MN 55414

**Mountain Club of Maryland**
6029 Lorley Beach Road
White Marsh, MD 21162

**The Mountaineers**
300 Third Avenue, W
Seattle, WA 98119

**Mount Rogers Appalachian Trail Club**
Route 7, Box 345
Abingdon, VA 24210

**Nantahala Hiking Club**
31 Carl Slagle Road
Franklin, NC 28734

**Natural Bridge Appalachian Trail Club**
P.O. Box 3012
Lynchburg, VA 24503

**New Hampshire Outing Club**
MUB Room 129
University of New Hampshire
Durham, NH 03824

**New Mexico Mountain Club**
119 Fortieth Street, NW
Albuquerque, NM 87105

**North Carolina Trails Association**
P.O. Box 1033
Greensboro, NC 27402

**North Country Trail Association**
P.O. Box 311
White Cloud, MI 49349

**New York/New Jersey Trail Conference**
232 Madison Avenue, Room 908
New York, NY 10016

**Old Dominion Appalachian Trail Club**
P.O. Box 25283
Richmond, VA 23260

**Ozark Highlands Trail Association**
411 Patricia Lane
Fayetteville, AR 72703

**Pacific Crest Trail Conference**
365 West Twenty-Ninth Avenue
Eugene, OR 97405

**Piedmont Appalachian Trail Hikers**
P.O. Box 4423
Greensboro, NC 27404

**Potomac Appalachian Trail Club**
1718 N Street, NW
Washington, DC 20036

**Penn State Outing Club**
Intramural Building, Room 4
University Park, PA 16802

**Roanoke Appalachian Trail Club**
P.O. Box 12282
Roanoke, VA 24024

**San Francisco Bay Area Ridge Trail Council**
116 New Montgomery Street, Suite 640
San Francisco, CA 94105

**Shenango Outing Club**
P.O. Box 244
Greenville, PA 16125

**Smoky Mountains Hiking Club**
P.O. Box 1454
Knoxville, TN 37901

**Southampton Trails Preservation Society**
P.O. Box 1172
Bridgehampton, NY 11932

**Southern Arizona Hiking Club**
P.O. Box 12122
Tucson, AZ 85732

**Superior Hiking Trail Association**
P.O. Box 2157
Tofte, MN 55615

**Susquehanna Appalachian Trail Club**
P.O. Box 215
Harrisburg, PA 17108

**Tahoe Rim Trail**
Westgate Professional Building
3170 Highway 50
P.O. Box 10156
South Lake Tahoe, CA 95731

**Taku Conservation Society**
1700 Branta Road
Juneau, AK 99801

**Tennessee Eastman Hiking Club**
P.O. Box 511
Kingsport, TN 37662

**Tidewater Appalachian Trail Club**
P.O. Box 8246
Norfolk, VA 23503

**Trail Center**
4898 El Camino Real, Office 205-A
Los Altos, CA 94022

**Trails Club of Rossmoor**
4139 Terra Grenada Drive, No. 18
Walnut Creek, CA 94595

**U.C. Mountaineering Club**
340 TUC
University of Cincinnati
Cincinnati, OH 45221

**Virginia Tech Outing Club**
P.O. Box 538
Blacksburg, VA 24060

**Virginia Trails Association**
13 Maple Street
Alexandria, VA 22301

**Volunteers for Outdoor Allegheny**
North Park Administration Building
Pearce Mill Road
Allison Park, PA 15101

**Volunteers for Outdoor Washington**
4516 University Way, NE
Seattle, WA 98105

**Volunteers for the Outdoors**
P.O. Box 36246
Albuquerque, NM 87176

**Vulcan Trail Association**
P.O. Box 19116
Birmingham, AL 35219

**Wanderbirds Hiking Club**
2001 Columbia Pike, No. 125
Arlington, VA 22204

**Washington Trails Association**
1305 Fourth Avenue, No. 518
Seattle, WA 98101

**West Texas Trail Walkers, Inc.**
1100 Wayland Drive
Arlington, TX 76012

**Wilmington Trail Club**
P.O. Box 1184
Wilmington, DE 19899

**Woodswomen**
25 West Diamond Lake Road
Minneapolis, MN 55419

# Bibliography

Allison, Linda. *The Wild Inside, the Sierra Club's Guide to the Great Indoors.* Sierra Club Books, 1979.

*The Big Bear Cub Scout Book.* Boy Scouts of America, 1991.

Birchard, William, Jr., and Robert D. Proudman. *Trail Design, Construction and Maintenance.* The Appalachian Trail Conference, 1981.

*Boy Scout Handbook*, 10th ed. Boy Scouts of America, 1990.

*Fieldbook*, 3d ed. Boy Scouts of America, 1984.

*Fifty Simple Things You Can Do to Save the Earth.* The Earthworks Group, 1989.

Kress, Stephen. *Audubon Society Guide to Attracting Birds.* New York: Charles Scribner's Sons, 1985.

Leopold, Aldo. *A Sand County Almanac.* Oxford University Press, 1966.

Lipkis, Andy and Katie. *The Simple Act of Planting a Tree.* Jeremy P. Tarcher, Inc., 1990.

Proudman, Robert D. and Reuben Rajala. *Trail Building and Maintenance.* 2d ed. Appalachian Mountain Club, 1981.

Stokes, Donald and Lillian. *The Bird Feeder Book.* Little, Brown, 1987.

Stokes, Donald and Lillian. *The Complete Birdhouse Book.* Little, Brown, 1990.

Shaffer, Carolyn and Erica Fielder. *City Safaris.* Sierra Club Books, 1987.

*Webelos Scout Book.* Boy Scouts of America, 1991.

*Wolf Cub Scout Book.* Boy Scouts of America, 1991.

Yates, Steve. *Adopting A Stream: A Northwest Handbook.* An Adopt-A-Stream Foundation Publication distributed by University of Washington Press, 1988.

# Index

## Illustrations

John Hunter—pages 32, 33, 69, 70, 71,
72, 73, 74, 75, 76, 77

Frank Bolle—pages 79, 81, 83, 84,
86,89

Colin Williams—pages 91, 92, 95

David Strand—page 109

## Photo Credits

Chris Michaels—pages 10, 25, 27, 50

Jay Addison Satz—page 85

Scott Stenjem—pages 37, 44, 89, 93,
102

Doug Wilson—page 58, 79